Salt
& Time

Recipes from a
Russian Kitchen

Alissa
Timoshkina

Salt & Time

Interlink Books

An imprint of Interlink Publishing Group, Inc.
Northampton, Massachusetts

In memory of my great-grandma, Rosalia, who showed
me that the act of feeding is the act of true love.

Introduction

We often need distance and time both to see things better and to feel closer to them. This is certainly true of the food of my home country, Russia—or Siberia, to be exact. When I think of that place, I can immediately hear the sound of fresh snow crunching beneath my feet. Having lived in England half of my life, this is what I miss the most about Russia: the clarity and stillness of the fresh fallen snow. It's a bit like a blank page on to which a new day can be drawn. Today, whenever I crush sea salt flakes between my fingers as I cook in my London kitchen, I think of that sound.

For many, Russian food remains a mystery, tinted with the stereotypes of the Cold War and obscured by the complexities of contemporary Russian politics. I often find that Russian cuisine is trapped somewhere between two very opposing ideas: the romanticized notion of Russians eating blinis with caviar every morning, and a stark image of Soviets gazing at bare market shelves to the soundtrack of their rumbling stomachs. So I feel it is finally time to paint a more authentic portrait. In this book, I would like to invite you to sit next to me at my Russian table, to share my memories of growing up in Siberia, and to accompany me on a journey across the vast country as well as into its fascinating history.

Born in the early 1980s in the industrial city of Omsk (famed for hosting Fyodor Dostoevsky during his exile), like many Siberians I come from a mixed heritage. Mine includes Jewish Ukrainian roots on my mom's side, my father's family comes from the Russian Far East, and we all share that unique experience of living under the Soviet regime. I never took much interest in my country until I moved away at aged 15 to receive the much-sought-after British education. The initial mist of home-longing was replaced by a more critical interest in Russia's history, culture, and politics. The more I delved into the academic world, the more acutely aware I became of the intricacies of my country's past, as well as of the dangerous trajectory of its current regime. While I have always loved Russian literature, classical music, and cinema, the political actualities of recent decades have left me feeling alienated. But, of course, it is from family that a sense of belonging really stems. Thinking of the variety of journeys that my family had made to settle in Siberia inspired a realization in me that there have been millions of other families traveling to the region from all over the former Soviet Union and beyond, bringing their ethnic, cultural, and culinary heritage along the way. And voilà—this is where my passion and interest in my home country was reignited.

Historically, Siberia was a place of exile from the mid-17th century until the 1950s. A vast region, it spans from the Ural Mountains eastwards to China, bordering Kazakhstan, Mongolia, and the Arctic Ocean. The sheer size of the place, and of Russia in general, is sometimes mind-boggling and sadly often used to stir up a false sense of patriotism and nationalistic pride. However, when seen through a culinary lens, the country's vastness is an asset and something to feel inspired by. Due to its complex history of exile and other forms of resettlement, Siberia has become a melting pot of culinary traditions from Ukraine and the Caucasus to Central Asia, Mongolia, and Korea.

The intense climate, with temperatures ranging from minus 40°F (40°C), to 104°F (40°C), doesn't make Siberia a land of plenty, and sadly I cannot recall growing up connected to the land and its produce—yet I can always remember the opulence of the markets in the summer, where the polyphony of the traders' accents was matched by the diversity of the foods on offer. There were Georgian spices and herbs next to a stall of Korean pickles, nudging up against dried fruits and spice mixes from Central Asia, not to mention freshly baked Armenian lavash breads and Ukrainian unrefined sunflower oil. While summers meant cooking and eating alfresco, the almost paralyzing cold of winter brought a profound indoor coziness and an entirely new set of food rituals. Vodka and pickles were brought out as soon as the first snow hit the ground, the scarcity of daylight outside was met with the warm glow of a dinner table lamp, and the need for sustenance was satisfied by giant bowls of steaming *pelmeni* dumplings and hearty soups with lots of bread and butter.

I will share many more memories with you in *Salt & Time*. But before I say more about what you will find in this book, a note on what will be excluded. To me, eating and cooking are a real aesthetic pleasure. I love honest, good food, but an elegantly dressed plate—and I don't mean elaborate haute cuisine fare—is equally important. Here I offer my own aesthetic take on Russian food, so I'm sorry if you were expecting to see *matryoshka*-shaped pepper grinders, colorful wooden spoons, and ornate crystal bowls filled with mayo-dressed salads. I feel it is time to move on and celebrate Russian food outside of its conventional visual codes. Giving myself some creative license, I will feature recipes ranging from Ashkenazi to Russian and Central Asian cuisines, as well as those that are authentic to Siberia alone, together with family classics and my own new interpretations of traditional flavor combinations. As I explore a wide range regionally, I also embrace and mix various historical periods. I have studied pre-Revolutionary Russian cookbooks and an array of Soviet-era publications, as well as some traditional culinary books published in the past 20 years in Russia and the West.

So, in *Salt & Time*, you will encounter dishes from both the pre-Revolutionary era and Soviet days that are given a contemporary touch. This book will hopefully strip away the patina of cultural stereotypes and political negativity to reveal a cuisine that is vibrant, nourishing, exciting and, above all, relevant, no matter the time or the place.

I do hope you enjoy your culinary journey, and *bon appétit*!
(Or "*prijatnogo appetita*," as they say in Russia.)

Alissa

Ingredients & *Pantry*

While most ingredients listed in this section can be found in stores in North America, or replaced with similar alternatives, I also wanted to share some recipes that are entirely unique, using ingredients only native to Russia and Siberia. So I very much hope to awaken the adventurous cook in you, inspiring you to go the extra mile in sourcing the more unusual produce.

Bird Cherry

Similar in appearance to elderflower trees, bird cherry trees blossom all over Russia in May and produce tiny dark berries in late August. These are pounded into a flour, which is used for making dough as well as pie fillings. While small in size, the berry has the most intense flavor that can be likened to a mixture of bitter almond and morello cherries. When used in a cake mix, the flour not only amplifies the flavor but also produces a gorgeous dark color and the loveliest grainy texture, similar to that of semolina and cornmeal. I don't offer any alternative recipe to the classic Bird Cherry Cake in the book (*see* page 196), since I very much hope you will be able to taste the original. See the Suppliers section on page 235.

Bread

Russians love their rye breads! Sourdough rye has been in their diet since before the Middle Ages, and continues to occupy an almost sacred place in the kitchen. Admittedly, the variety of breads is rather limited, with the most poplar ones being a simple rye bread (aka Russian rye) and a fragrant *Borodinsky* studded with whole coriander and caraway seeds. Luckily, in recent years, some North American bakeries have started producing these gorgeous loaves—*see* Suppliers, page 235.

Buckwheat

It would not be an exaggeration to say that buckwheat is a key ingredient in Russian cuisine. It is mainly used in *kasha*, a sweet or savory porridge, as well as in stuffings for roast meats and pies, but is also milled into flour. Very popular in the West these days for its nutritional properties, in the Soviet era raw buckwheat was roasted on an industrial scale as a way to preserve it. While some of its nutritional value was depleted in the process, the buckwheat acquired the most beautiful nutty flavor and texture. This is the type of buckwheat many Soviet generations, including myself, grew up with, so throughout the book I am referring to roasted buckwheat only.

Edible Fiddlehead Ferns

This is one of most unique and wonderful culinary ingredients that I was lucky to have grown up eating. There exists numerous varieties of ferns all over the world, most of which are commonly known as wild and house plants. However, experienced foragers will tell you that some fern plants, when at their earliest fiddlehead stage, make the most incredible cooking ingredient. The type of fern that I refer to in the book (*see* page 135) is *Osmunda japonica* that is found in the Russian Far East, Japan, China, Korea, and Taiwan. Ostrich fern (*Matteuccia struthiopteris*) is a type commonly found in North America, but is only in season for a short while in early spring. Make sure to do some research and consult a forager before you source your edible ferns.

Herring

While herring is commonly associated with Scandinavian cuisine, it has been a staple of Russian cuisine, too. Found in the Barents Sea, which neighbors the Norwegian Sea, Russian herring is always preserved in salt brine and spices. So it is of paramount importance (and I am not exaggerating here) that you use the Russian-style salt and spice brined herring and not the Scandinavian kind preserved in vinegar and sugar when cooking from this book (*see* Suppliers, page 235).

Sea Buckthorn

This humble bush berry, native to Siberia, also grows in parts of North America and can be obtained from experienced foragers. Rich in nutritional values, it has a unique taste—a mix between orange zest and juicy apricot. The use of sea buckthorn in Russian cuisine is endless, from *mors* drink (*see* page 225) and tea and vodka infusions to jams and jellies. I can't think of any berry or fruit that could make a worthy alternative to sea buckthorn, so do find a way to treat yourself to the authentic flavor of this little orange berry (*see* Suppliers, page 235).

Smetana

As you will see, sour cream, or *smetana* in Russian, appears on pretty much every page of this book. It contributes a unique creamy and tangy flavor to any dish, from salad dressings to cake mixtures and frostings. There are countless varieties of smetana in Russia, ranging from standard supermarket brands with an average fat content of 15% to the most luscious farmers' market smetana as rich in fat as 40%. I usually tend to use the creamiest smetana for savory dishes, such as fermented soups, while light and tangy smetana makes an amazing dessert ingredient to add an extra level of flavor complexity and freshness. Use standard sour cream, crème fraîche, or go the extra mile to an Eastern European food store and buy yourself a jar of the real deal.

Spices

Russian

While there are no specific spices that are used in Russian cuisine alone, black pepper, coriander, caraway, and fennel seeds are absolutely key. Throughout this book you will find a whole range of recipes, from desserts to ferments, that use either one or the whole selection of these spices. I would strongly encourage you to use the freshest kind available and toast them first before using whole, crushing, or grinding into a powder. The aroma and flavor complexity that these yield is unparalleled.

Korean

The spices used in the Soviet-Korean recipes throughout the book are quite different from the authentic ones you would find in any modern Korean cookbooks. Adapted to Russian palates, these spices are a lot milder and incorporate classic Russian flavors such as coriander seeds. You will find a recipe for Soviet-Korean spice mix on page 166, but if you don't have all the ingredients you can just use freshly toasted and coarsely ground coriander seeds and cayenne pepper, since these are the main flavor notes of any Soviet-Korean dish.

Sunflower Oil

Sunflowers are one of the most common oil seed crops throughout the former Soviet territories. The original unrefined oil, which has nothing in common with the flavorless refined type used widely for cooking, is characterized by a deep golden color and an incredible aroma of toasted seeds. Sold at farmers' markets by weight, it is never used for cooking, but only to drizzle on fresh salads in the summer or on a selection of ferments in winter. While it is impossible to find the original farmers' market oil in North America, you can buy flavorful sunflower oil from any Eastern European shop—just make sure to get an unrefined type. Alternatively, the UK brand Clearspring makes its own organic sunflower oil, which is equally good for cooking and drizzling (*see* Suppliers, page 235).

Tvorog

Tvorog and smetana go together like a burger and fries. A Slavic relative of cottage cheese, tvorog is a type of dairy product obtained by curdling milk with sour cream or kefir. Traditionally, tvorog, mixed with smetana, is eaten on its own for breakfast as well as used in a whole range of sweet bakes and desserts (*see* pages 176 and 181), but do give it a try in savory dishes, too (*see* page 20).

Unshelled Pine Nuts

Siberian forests are abundant with pine trees and so the regional cuisine is filled with the rich flavors of the nuts, both shelled and unshelled. Usually sold at markets by weight, unshelled pine nuts are used in various infusions, be it honey, tea, or vodka. While this type of pine nut is hard to find in North America, I wanted to share one recipe in this book so as to give an example of a peculiar Siberian culinary tradition (*see* page 233).

Appetizers, Sides & Salads

Chapter 1

While you might think that the title of this chapter refers to three different types of dishes, in Russian cuisine it can be a single plate that encompasses all three functions. Russian salads are not the light, leafy-green creations that we are accustomed to in the West. Usually rich with mayo, root vegetables, and some type of protein, these would stand firmly as an appetizer, if not a main course. The Slavic tradition of feasting also requires that all appetizers, salads, and side dishes are brought out in a glorious bunch to begin the meal and that these plates and bowls don't leave the table until the dessert arrives—sometimes not even then. While I rarely eat this way when cooking at home, I do tend to over-order in restaurants, since the sight of just one plate in front of me can bring a sense of inexplicable sadness (often a source of annoyance for my partner, whose British-South African upbringing makes him marvel at my need to have at least three plates on the table at a time). In this chapter I present a wide range of dishes that do work really well on their own, or when served in a more traditional "course after course" meal. But I would really encourage you to stage a Russian family-style feast: bring out lots of dishes to the table to truly indulge the eye and the palate.

Rye Crostini *Three Ways*

A more elegant take on a classic Russian welcome snack, these crostini taste as good as they look. Welcoming someone to your home with bread and salt is a very old Slavic tradition that has survived into the present-day language. Although no one greets their guests with a large chunk of bread and a small bowl of salt anymore, saying that someone gave you a "bread and salt" welcome means you were treated very generously by your hosts. These recipes are inspired by the old Russian tradition, cobbling together some of the classic flavor combinations, such as rye bread, butter, dill, beets, and scallions, while throwing in a few unorthodox flavors, too. Feel free to experiment, swapping various ingredients around or inventing your very own Russian-style crostini.

Dill Butter, Radishes & Charred Scallions

SERVES 4–8

—

4 slices of dark rye or
　Borodinsky bread
　(*see* page 12)
7 tablespoons (3½ oz/100 g)
　unsalted butter, softened
2 large pinches of sea salt
　flakes, plus extra to serve
3½ oz (100 g) dill, roughly
　chopped
8 scallions, roughly chopped
2 tablespoons unrefined
　sunflower oil
8 radishes

Lightly toast the bread on a dry nonstick frying pan or in a toaster. Set aside to cool down.

Using a small food processor or a handheld immersion blender, blend the butter with the salt and dill until a light fluffy green paste is achieved. This should not take more than 2 minutes.

Place a grill pan over high heat. Lightly brush the scallions with the oil before placing them on the hot pan. Char for about 1 minute on each side or as long as it takes for the distinct grill marks to appear.

Wash the radishes (remove the leaves if they are still attached) and slice into thin discs.

To serve, smother each slice of toasted bread with about a tablespoon of the dill butter. Cut each in half if serving 8 people as canapés, or leave the slices whole if serving as an appetizer. Top with the charred scallions, which you can curve into an appealing shape, and dot over the discs of radish. Add a final sprinkle of salt before serving.

Tarragon *Tvorog*, Roasted Beets & Pickled Grapes

—

scant ½ cup (100 ml) red wine
   vinegar

3½ tablespoons water

finely grated zest and juice
   of 1 lemon

1 small hot red chili pepper,
   halved

2 teaspoons brown sugar

handful of red seedless grapes

2 raw red beets, washed

1 tablespoon olive oil, plus
   extra for dressing the beets

small bunch of tarragon,
   leaves only

1 cup (7 oz/200 g) tvorog
   (see page 14), farmer
   cheese, or cottage cheese

4 slices of dark rye or
   Borodinsky bread (*see*
   page 12)

sea salt flakes

Start by making the pickled grapes. To prepare the brine, in a small non-reactive bowl, mix together the vinegar, measured water, half of the lemon zest and juice (reserve the remainder for the cheese), the chili pepper, sugar, and a pinch of sea salt flakes.

Cut each grape in half and add to the brine. Give the mixture a stir, cover with plastic wrap, and put into the refrigerator to pickle while you get busy with the rest of the dish.

To roast the beets, preheat the oven to 425°F (220°C). Place the whole beets on a roasting pan, brush them with the olive oil, and sprinkle them with sea salt. Cover with foil and roast for 40 minutes or until they can be pierced easily but still retain a bit of crunch.

To peel the beets, let them cool down, then simply pinch the skin, which should come off easily. Cut each beet into medium-sized wedges (roughly 8 per beet), dress with a little olive oil and salt, and set aside.

Finely chop the tarragon leaves (reserving a few to garnish), then mix them with the tvorog (or farmer or cottage cheese), add the remaining lemon zest and juice, and season with salt. Give it a good mix and taste to adjust the seasoning.

To assemble the crostini, toast the bread as on page 18. Cut in half if serving 8 people as canapés, or leave the slices whole if serving as an appetizer. Top each slice with a heaped tablespoon of the tvorog mixture, followed by a wedge of roasted beet and 1 or 2 pickled grape halves. Garnish with the reserved tarragon leaves and a few sea salt flakes.

Russian Dukkah Butter
with Fennel Tops

Dukkah is an Egyptian spice and nut mix widely used in Middle Eastern cuisine, and an absolute must in my pantry. Here I use a blend of seeds common in Eastern European cuisines to Russify one of my favorite condiments.

To make the dukkah, place a medium-sized frying pan over medium heat, add all the seeds and the peppercorns—in batches, if necessary to avoid overcrowding the pan—and toast for 3–5 minutes until they release their aroma, tossing them around in the pan. Transfer to paper towels to cool down. Roughly crush the spices in small batches using a mortar and pestle or an electric coffee grinder, making sure they remain very textural and do not turn into a powder. Add the salt and mix all the elements together.

The amount of spice mix you add to your butter really depends on your personal taste. In my view, you need at least 2 heaped teaspoons to create a deeply flavored spread. Using a small food processor or a handheld immersion blender, whizz the butter with the spice mix and sea salt flakes for about 1 minute.

To serve, toast the bread as on page 18. Cut in half if serving 8 people as canapés, or leave the slices whole if serving as an appetizer. Smother each with a very generous amount of the butter—remember it is the star of the show and not just a base ingredient. Add a finishing touch to each slice with a little extra pinch of dukkah and a few sprigs of fennel fronds.

This canapé works equally well when the butter is served hummus-style with a side of toasted bread for dipping. Make sure the butter has been at room temperature for several hours. Do not blend it with the dukkah, but just smear it around a plate or a shallow bowl, then top it with 2–4 tablespoons of the dukkah and scatter around the fennel fronds.

SERVES 4–8

—

7 tablespoons (3½ oz/100 g)
   unsalted butter, softened
1 teaspoon sea salt flakes
4 slices of rye bread
handful of fennel fronds

For the dukkah
2 teaspoons fennel seeds
2 teaspoons coriander seeds
½ teaspoon caraway seeds
2 teaspoons sunflower seeds
2 teaspoons black
   peppercorns
1 teaspoon salt

Zucchini Dip

Similar to that ultimate classic, eggplant caviar (or Babushka Ganoush, *see* page 38), the zucchini dip has an almost sacred place in every (former) Soviet heart. Typically sold in glass jars, the dip has been consumed by the Soviets for generations. However, while sometimes indulging my childhood nostalgia for the yellowy brown paste, I often struggle to taste the difference between the different types of Soviet vegetable dip, since they essentially use the same base of tomatoes, carrots, onions, and garlic. So here I offer my own take on the original, letting the zucchini shine through while still drawing on the traditional flavors of dill and sour cream to honor its Slavic origin.

Heat up 2 tablespoons of the oil in a medium saucepan, add the onions and garlic with a pinch of salt, and fry over medium heat for 10–15 minutes until the onions become translucent and start to melt together. Transfer to a bowl.

Add the remaining tablespoon of oil to the pan and let it heat up, then add the zucchinis with a pinch of salt and stir through. Cook, uncovered, for 30 minutes or until the zucchinis have softened and released their liquid. If there is quite a lot of it, strain it off before adding the seasonings: the dried mint, fresh dill, and a pinch of pepper.

Let the vegetables cool down, then use a food processor or a handheld immersion blender to whizz with the sour cream or yogurt into a paste. If you prefer a chunkier texture, whisk the zucchinis vigorously with a fork while they are still hot and then add the sour cream or yogurt. Taste for seasoning and add more salt and pepper as necessary.

Sprinkle with some extra dill, drizzle with sunflower oil, and serve with warm bread.

SERVES 4

—

3 tablespoons good-quality unrefined sunflower oil, plus extra to serve

2 onions, finely diced

2–3 garlic cloves, grated

3 zucchinis, sliced into semi-circles

½ teaspoon dried mint

3 tablespoons chopped dill, plus extra to serve

3 tablespoons sour cream or Greek yogurt

salt and freshly ground black pepper

Crab Salad *with* Charred Corn

SERVES 4

—

For the pea purée

1¾ cups (9 oz/250 g)
  defrosted frozen peas

1 small garlic clove, grated

½ teaspoon red pepper flakes

1 teaspoon salt

finely grated zest and juice
  of 1 lime

1 tablespoon olive oil

For the pickled relish

scant ½ cup (100 ml) white
  wine vinegar

1 small garlic clove, grated

1 tablespoon clear honey

1 teaspoon salt

½ large cucumber, finely diced

½ green dessert apple, cored
  and finely diced

For the charred corn

1 cup (5½ oz/160 g) drained
  canned corn, or 2 large ears
  of corn (when in season)

1 tablespoon olive oil

1 teaspoon sea salt flakes

For the crab meat

4 heaped tablespoons
  white crab meat

juice of ½ lemon

pinch of salt

handful of cilantro leaves,
  to garnish

Ever since the first surimi production factory opened in the Russian city of Murmansk in the early 1980s, virtually no Soviet kid was left untouched by the crab sticks craze. Rapidly becoming a favorite national ingredient, the processed fish substance compressed into pink "sticks" was used in a variety of "crab salads," usually containing rice, cucumber, corn, peas, apples, and—yes, you guessed it—mayo! While most of the Soviet Union had to make do with the surimi substitute, my dad's family along with the rest of the population of the Russian Far East had access to fresh crab meat, particularly that of the Kamchatka crab, and could enjoy *real* crab salad in all its glory. Luckily, I have recovered from my childhood obsession with fake crab sticks and have developed this recipe using authentic crab meat and some of the original ingredients from the classic Soviet salad.

This dish is a stunning appetizer with which to wow your guests, or it can be served as part of a mezze-style salad spread. At a recent dinner party it worked really well alongside rye bread with Russian Dukkah Butter (*see* page 21), so give that a try.

Make the pea purée by blending all the ingredients together in a food processor, then pass the purée through a sieve to achieve a silky smooth consistency. Set aside.

To make the pickled relish, prepare the pickling brine by mixing together the vinegar, garlic, honey, and salt in a non-reactive bowl, stirring well to dissolve the garlic as much as possible. Add the cucumber and apple to a clean small jar, pour over the pickling brine, and cover with the lid, then leave in the refrigerator for 30 minutes–1 hour.

If using canned corn, pat it dry with paper towels. Spread evenly on a roasting pan, drizzle with the olive oil, and sprinkle with the sea salt. Place under a preheated broiler for 10 minutes or until the corn starts to blacken and pop in places. If using corn on the cob, brush with the oil and sprinkle with the salt. Cook under the broiler for 5–8 minutes on each side until charred. Cut the corn kernels from the cobs and set aside.

When ready to serve the salad, dress the crab with the lemon juice and salt. Place a heaped tablespoon of pea purée in the middle of each plate and spread it into an even circle. Add a heaped tablespoon of the crab meat to the center and an equal amount of charred corn scattered on top of it. Drain the excess pickling juice from the cucumber and apple, then scatter the cubes around the circumference of each plate (if using round plates). Finally, drop a few cilantro leaves on to the plate.

Cured Fish: A Summer Classic

You know summer has arrived in Siberia when sterlet appears on your table. Oven-roasted or barbecued, this white fish—which comes from the sturgeon family—is an absolute must in my parents' household. Found in most rivers in Siberia, sterlet was very popular among the Russian tsars, who consumed it in many guises, and most famously as a rather expensive and tricky dish: a pie stuffed with sterlet spines. Never fans of unnecessarily expensive and tricky dishes (I mean, we are not tsars anyway), my family usually opts for a simple summer classic of quick-cured sterlet. Sadly, over the years sterlet have become critically endangered, so we've come up with the next best thing—cured mackerel. Requiring nothing more than salt, a few herbs, and a little bit of time, the cured fish is a perfect nibble at a summer barbecue alongside a cold beer.

Gut and thoroughly wash the fish, or ask the fishmonger to do so. In a small bowl, mix the salt and sugar.

Place both fish on a sheet of foil or parchment paper and generously rub with the salt and sugar mixture, inside and out. Stuff the insides with seasonal herbs, tie tightly with twine, and wrap in the foil or parchment paper. Place in a plastic food bag or a bowl to prevent any leakage, and leave in the refrigerator for 48 hours.

To serve your mackerel, remove the bag, foil or parchment paper, twine, and all the herbs, and cut across the body into ¾ inch (2 cm) chunks, discarding the head and tail, if desired. Dress with an extra sprinkle of salt and more fresh herbs. Make sure to serve alongside a large stack of napkins, since this will be a deliciously messy affair.

SERVES 4–6

—

2 mackerel (each 9–10½ oz/ 250–300 g)

4 tablespoons coarse sea salt, plus extra to serve

2 tablespoons sugar

a bundle of fresh herbs, such as dill, cilantro, thyme, rosemary, purple basil, plus extra to serve

Vegetable Patties *with* Dipping Sauces

Patties, or *kotlety*, are a go-to dish in most Russian households. Usually made from ground meat, there are also vegetarian alternatives, the most popular being beet, cabbage with potato, and carrot. Often consumed in our family as an after-school snack, I'll forever associate these patties with a grocery store in Omsk called "Ocean." Specializing in fish and seafood, as you have probably guessed from its name, the supermarket also sold my favorite vegetable patties. Conveniently, it was situated halfway between my home and my school. The walk to school was particularly arduous each winter, with temperatures on dark, windy mornings plunging below minus 4°F (minus 20°C). Passing through the back alley behind the store, my mom and I would always get a waft of warm fishy air coming from its extractor fan. And each time that brief moment of warmth (despite the unpleasant smell) and a comforting flash-forward to our journey back from school with a bundle of vegetable patties gave me strength for the second leg of the ice-cold walk. The versions offered here are my improvisations on the three popular flavors.

Beet Patties *with* Horseradish Cream

SERVES 4–6

—

For the patties

2 large raw red beets, peeled and grated

¼ cup (1½ oz/40 g) fine semolina, plus a few tablespoons for coating

2 garlic cloves, grated

2 handfuls of walnuts, roughly chopped

2 handfuls of dill, finely chopped

1 egg, lightly beaten

2 generous pinches of salt

pinch of toasted and freshly ground black peppercorns

sunflower oil, for shallow frying

Mix together all the ingredients for the patties (except the oil for frying) in a large bowl, and season with salt and pepper as I have suggested, or to your own taste.

Feel free to decide on the size of your patties: traditionally, these are made in the size of a medium burger patty, but I prefer to make them smaller and serve on a platter at a finger-food buffet or as part of a sharing *zakuski*-style (mezze-like) dinner. For the smaller version, take a heaped tablespoon of the mixture for each, roll it into a ball between your hands, and then flatten it slightly. Sprinkle each side with some semolina.

To shallow-fry the patties, you will need 4–6 tablespoons of oil, but the exact amount, of course, will depend on the size of your frying pan. Before adding the patties, make sure the oil is hot enough. You can always do a test by lowering a teaspoon of the mixture into the oil—you will know it's ready to go when the mixture starts sizzling straight away. Cook for 3–5 minutes on each side until lightly browned, then lay out on paper towels to absorb the excess oil, and cool to room temperature.

For the horseradish cream
1–2 tablespoons peeled and
    grated fresh horseradish
    root
6 heaped tablespoons crème
    fraîche
2 teaspoons white wine
    vinegar
finely grated zest and juice of
    ½ lemon
salt and freshly ground
    black pepper

To make the horseradish cream, choose the amount of horseradish according to your personal pleasure-pain threshold and mix with the crème fraîche, vinegar, and lemon zest and juice, then season to taste. A pinch of salt and pepper will do, I believe.

Serve the patties on a platter with a small bowl of horseradish cream placed in the middle, or individually plated with some bread and a simple green salad.

Potato & Sauerkraut Patties *with* Dill Sour Cream & Crispy Shallots

PICTURED ON PAGE 29

SERVES 4–6

—

For the patties

4 white floury potatoes,
    such as Russets

4 heaped tablespoons white
    sauerkraut, drained of brine

¼ cup (1½ oz/40 g) fine
    semolina, plus a few
    tablespoons for coating

1 egg, lightly beaten

salt and freshly ground
    black pepper

sunflower oil, for shallow-
    frying

For the crispy shallots

2 banana shallots

2 teaspoons all-purpose flour

salt and freshly ground
    black pepper

sunflower oil, for shallow-
    frying

For the dill sour cream

6 heaped tablespoons
    sour cream

2 heaped tablespoons
    chopped dill

small pinch of salt

Peel and cut the potatoes into evenly sized chunks. Place in a large pot of cold water with a large pinch of salt and bring to a boil. It is essential to cook the potatoes until just soft but not mushy, since we really don't need any excess water in the patties. This should take about 10 minutes. Once cooked to the right texture, drain thoroughly and get rid of any extra liquid by returning the pot with the drained potatoes to the heat for a minute.

Crush the potatoes using a fork, since you want an uneven texture with some chunks still intact. Add the sauerkraut, semolina, and egg, along with a few pinches of salt and pepper, and mix to combine.

Shape the patties to your liking: for generous medium-sized ones, you will need a palmful of the mixture for each, or make smaller ones using a heaped tablespoon for each. Sprinkle each side with semolina.

Follow the same method to fry as for Beet Patties (*see* page 28).

In the meantime, to make the crispy shallots, peel and then slice them into medium-thin rounds using a mandolin. If slicing by hand, make sure you use a sharp knife and cut as evenly as you can.

Mix the flour with some salt and pepper, then coat each shallot round in the seasoned flour. Heat a shallow depth of oil until hot, then fry the shallots for 3–4 minutes, flipping them over halfway through. The shallots should be crisp and acquire a pleasant amber color, but must not burn or they will taste bitter.

Mix the ingredients for the dill sour cream together, but just remember that the sauerkraut will make the patties quite salty, so the sauce won't need much seasoning.

I like serving these individually plated as an appetizer: smear the dill sour cream across the plate (preferably a dark-colored one to make a beautifully contrasting effect), place one patty on top, and crown with a teaspoon of crispy shallots.

Carrot Patties *with* Coriander Yogurt

In a large bowl, mix together all the ingredients for the patties (except the oil for frying) and add salt to taste.

While before I suggested optional sizes for the patties, I would encourage you to make these bite-sized, using a heaped tablespoon for each. Sprinkle each side with semolina.

Follow the same method to fry them as for the Beet Patties (*see* page 28).

The key to a very flavorful dip is using freshly ground toasted coriander seeds as opposed to ready-ground coriander. While you will only need 2 tablespoons here, I recommend preparing a whole batch that you can then use for other recipes. Heat up a medium-sized frying pan over medium heat, add 3 palmfuls of coriander seeds (don't overcrowd the pan, since they need to toast evenly) and toast for 3–5 minutes, tossing them around in the pan—you will know the process is underway when the seeds start releasing a dizzying aroma. Transfer to paper towels to cool down. Roughly crush the seeds in small batches using a mortar and pestle or an electric coffee grinder.

Mix 2 tablespoons of the freshly ground seeds with the yogurt and salt.

PICTURED ON PAGE 29

SERVES 4–6

—

For the patties

4 carrots, peeled and grated

2 tablespoons finely chopped dried apricots

¼ cup (1½ oz/40 g) semolina, plus a few tablespoons for coating

2 eggs, lightly beaten

½ teaspoon cayenne pepper

salt

sunflower oil, for shallow-frying

For the coriander yogurt

2 tablespoons toasted and roughly crushed coriander seeds (*see* method)

6 tablespoons good-quality Greek yogurt

small pinch of salt

Khe
Soviet-Korean Ceviche

MAKES 4

—

9 oz (250 g) skinless cod loin
    from a sustainable source
sesame or unrefined sunflower
    oil, for drizzling

For the marinade
¼ teaspoon cayenne pepper
½ teaspoon salt
1 teaspoon sugar
1 teaspoon fish sauce
2 teaspoons sesame oil
finely grated zest and juice
    of 1 lemon
1 garlic clove, grated
½ cup (120 ml) white wine
    vinegar

For the salad
2 tablespoons sunflower oil
½ onion, thinly sliced
pinch of salt
2 tablespoons coriander
    seeds, toasted and freshly
    ground (*see* page 31)
1 large carrot, peeled and
    grated

To garnish
cilantro leaves
white sesame seeds

A good example of the diverse culinary influences that form Russian cuisine, *khe* is a dish that originates from the far east of the country, where a large Korean population—known as *Koryo-saram*—has been living for generations. Arriving in the former Russian Empire in the 19th century, Korean migrants settled in the Far East and Siberia, then gradually moved further south, integrating and adapting their culinary heritage along the way. This dish, as with others in Soviet-Korean cuisine, features a signature combination of acid, salt, sugar, and chili, while sunflower oil and coriander remind us of its dual identity. Originally made with Sakhalin taimen, a species of fish from the salmon family that has sadly become endangered, these days *khe* is usually made with cod or carp, but I would also encourage you to try this with squid and other types of seafood.

First prepare the marinade in which the cod will be "cooked." Mix all the ingredients together in a large non-reactive bowl and let them infuse while you prepare the cod. Traditionally the fish is cut into chunks, but I prefer thin strips. You will need to use a sharp knife to cut the cod loin lengthways into strips as thinly as you can. Once ready, place the cod in the bowl of marinade, mix well, and keep it entirely submerged in the liquid by placing a small plate with a cup of water, or anything else heavy, on top. Refrigerate for 30 minutes to an hour.

    Meanwhile, prepare the carrot salad. Heat the oil in a frying pan and fry the onion with the salt over medium heat for about 7 minutes until it has become translucent, then add the ground coriander seeds, mix well, and remove from the heat. Stir in the grated carrot and let the mixture cool completely.

    Once the fish is ready, drain off the marinade and add the contents of the carrot pan to the bowl with the cod. Mix well and season with a drizzle of sesame or sunflower oil (depending on which flavor profile of the dish you want to bring out more, Asian or Slavic). You can serve this in individual bowls or as a large sharing plate—just make sure to garnish with some cilantro and a sprinkle of white sesame seeds.

Buckwheat *Vinegret* Salad

MAKES 4

—

1¼ cups (7 oz/200 g) roasted
buckwheat (*see* page 12)

1 cup (250 ml) salted boiling
water

¼ cup (60 ml) good-quality
unrefined sunflower oil, plus
extra for stirring through the
buckwheat and cooking the
beets

2 raw red beets, washed

1¾ cups (9 oz/250 g) frozen
peas

2 Fermented Cucumbers
(*see* page 152)

¼ cup (60 ml) Red Sauerkraut
with Garlic & Chili brining
liquid (*see* page 159) or brine
from your store-bought
sauerkraut

1–2 garlic cloves, grated

small bunch of dill,
finely chopped

1 tablespoon chopped
tarragon leaves

small bunch of parsley,
chopped

squeeze of lemon juice

salt and freshly ground
black pepper

Many popular Soviet dishes have their roots in pre-Revolutionary French-inspired cuisine. *Vinegret* is one of them. Born in the 18th century as a dish of diced game, boiled vegetables, and a classic French vinaigrette, this salad takes its title from the transliterated name of its dressing. A number of pre-Revolutionary dishes were simplified and popularized during the Soviet days, and so vinegret turned into a salad of boiled root vegetables dressed in sunflower oil. The acidity of the original French dressing was replaced (rather successfully in my view) with the sharpness of fermented cucumber and cabbage. Not all Soviet-era food alterations were as bad as popular opinion would have us believe. Although I do love the dish in its original Soviet form, I find it a bit too similar to the rest of the usual suspects in the Soviet salad family that contain boiled carrots and potatoes. So I've created my own version, which replaces some of the ingredients with soft herbs and buckwheat to give a bit of vibrancy, body, and texture, while retaining the signature briny sharpness.

To cook the buckwheat, simply place it in a saucepan and pour over the salted boiling water, cover with a lid, and leave to stand overnight, or simmer over a gentle heat for about 10 minutes until all the liquid is absorbed. Stir in a bit of oil and set aside.

Preheat the oven to 425°F (220°C). Drizzle the beets with sunflower oil, wrap in foil, and roast. You want them to lose their intense earthy bitterness, but they still need to retain a bit of a crunch, so 30–40 minutes should suffice, depending on their size. Defrost the peas by placing them in a colander and pouring some boiling water over them. Finely dice the fermented cucumbers.

To make the dressing, you will need to extract ¼ cup (60 ml) brining liquid from your jar of sauerkraut, then mix it with the sunflower oil and garlic, stirring well so the garlic dissolves as much as possible. Taste and add some salt if you feel it needs more.

Once the beets are ready (pierce the middle with a knife to check), let them cool down before peeling and cutting into wedges. I like mine quite chunky, since you really get to taste their meaty earthiness that way.

Mix all the ingredients together, adding the dill, tarragon, parsley, lemon juice, and the dressing to complete the dish.

Babushka Ganoush

—

2 tablespoons good-quality
    unrefined sunflower oil

1 onion, diced

2 garlic cloves, grated, plus an
    extra clove if you like

1 carrot, peeled and grated

1 red pepper, cored, deseeded,
    and cubed

¼ cup (60 ml) tomato paste

generous ¾ cup (200 ml)
    boiling water

1–2 teaspoons sweet chili
    sauce

2 eggplants, cubed

1 tablespoon each chopped
flat-leaf parsley, dill, and
    cilantro, plus extra sprigs
    to garnish

salt and freshly ground
    black pepper

sour cream, to garnish
    (optional)

Aka eggplant caviar, this is arguably one of the most widespread dishes in former Soviet countries, and is prepared in a different way by each household. In our family, it's my grandma Valentina who holds the title of the eggplant caviar expert. It must be the addition of chili sauce that makes her version a winner! Not so long ago, we took my grandmother out for dinner to a Lebanese restaurant for the first time in her life. Studying the menu, she became particularly fascinated by the (peculiar sounding to the Russian ear) dish baba ganoush. When I explained to her that it's pretty much the Middle Eastern equivalent of her good old eggplant caviar, my mom immediately came up with a new moniker for my gran: Babushka Ganoush. So it's fitting to use that whimsical name for this recipe belonging to my *babushka*, who is still the queen of the humble eggplant dip in our family.

Heat the oil in a medium saucepan and add the onion and garlic. Season with a pinch of salt and cook over medium heat for 5–8 minutes.

Add the carrot and red pepper, mix well, and cook for a further 5–7 minutes. I prefer to add a pinch of salt with every new batch of vegetables, but if you prefer your food less salty or are watching your salt intake, then skip the addition of salt here.

Dilute the tomato paste in a small bowl with the measured boiling water and add the chili sauce. Mix well and pour it over the vegetables. Give them another stir and bring to a simmer.

Add the eggplants with another pinch of salt. Mix all the vegetables to ensure that the eggplant cubes are evenly coated, reduce the heat, and let the caviar stew for 20–30 minutes, stirring regularly to prevent it sticking to the base of the pan. You will know it's ready when the eggplant starts to fall apart and all the vegetables begin to blend in easily when mixed around with a wooden spoon. At this point, you can add another clove of freshly crushed garlic, together with the herbs and pepper, if you would like to give the dish an extra kick.

Remove from the heat, cover the pan, and let it sit for 20 minutes or so as it cools down.

Depending on your personal taste, you can either serve the caviar chunky or turn it into a spread by mixing it all together with a handheld immersion blender. Serve as an appetizer dish or as part of a *zakuski*-style feast, garnished with a dollop of sour cream and some fresh herb sprigs, along with the obligatory rye bread, although the preferred serving method in our family is to eat it cold as a late-evening snack with some leftover mashed potatoes.

Lavash Wrap

MAKES 1 WRAP; ENOUGH FOR
2 TO SHARE

—

2 tablespoons finely
chopped dill

2 tablespoons finely
chopped cilantro

2 tablespoons finely chopped
flat-leaf parsley

4 heaped tablespoons Soviet-
Korean Pickled Carrots
(see page 166)

¾ cup (3½ oz/100 g) grated
Georgian Suluguni cheese
(see page 235), or ⅓ cup
(1¾ oz/50 g) crumbled feta
cheese mixed with ½ cup
(1¾ oz/50 g) grated
mozzarella cheese

1 Armenian lavash bread, or
2 tortillas, if lavash is not
available

1 tablespoon mild vegetable
oil, for grilling

This recipe belongs to my inventive mama, who unwittingly created a quintessentially Soviet dish, since this wrap quite literally embraces various national cuisines of the former USSR. Soviet-Korean Pickled Carrots (see page 166), a staple across the former Soviet Union, often make their appearance in dishes as varied as Georgian kebab wraps, Soviet "doctor's sausage" sandwiches, or in a popular post-Soviet street-food snack, hotdogs with mayo. So the wrap I present here is in a way a combination of all three. It can be devoured for lunch on its own, or served as part of a barbecue feast.

If you can, grill it on an open fire to add a bit of a smoky profile; but if an open fire is not available, char the wrap on a grill or griddle pan to get those gorgeous marks. As much as I enjoy its flavor and texture, it's the visual vibrancy of the dish that never fails to seduce me!

In a large bowl, mix together the fresh herbs, Soviet-Korean pickled carrots, and cheese.

Lay the lavash bread on an even work surface. Please note that if you are using tortillas, which are a lot smaller in size, make 2 sandwiches, dividing the filling between them. Spoon the contents of the bowl on to the lavash (or tortillas) and spread it out evenly, then roll into a burrito-shaped wrap.

Preheat a griddle pan over a high heat, brush the wrap with the oil and grill for 1–2 minutes on each side, to obtain the char marks and let the cheese soften.

Cut in half and share with your companion, or devour the whole thing. I won't judge you!

Pirozhki Stuffed Buns

Pirozhki is a word pretty much synonymous with the word *babushka*. I would struggle to find any Russian kid who didn't go to visit their grandma for a meal of freshly baked or fried stuffed buns and tea. While the tradition of eating pirozhki out of your granny's loving hands is firmly ingrained in Russian popular culture, these hot buns stuffed with all kinds of fillings were also a widespread street food in Soviet days. And guess what, the vendor would more often than not be a babushka. Sold on street corners and in underground stations, the buns would be wrapped in grey paper, stained with their oil. They were not the safest thing to consume—there was a lot of speculation as to the nature of their fillings, and rather crude expressions such as "pirozhki with nails" or—

worse yet—"pirozhki with kittens" entered the everyday lexicon. So let's return to the warm and, most importantly, safe environment of our babushka's kitchen to enjoy the pillowy, squeaky dough filled with such delightful ingredients as mushrooms, sauerkraut, cabbage and boiled eggs, or ground meat and onions. Below I offer some traditional recipes as well as a few improvisations to mix things up a little. Make sure to have a large cup of sweet black tea or steaming chicken broth (*see* page 90) in your hand when you settle down to consume your pirozhki.

The recipe for the dough belongs to my late paternal grandma Baba Toma (short for Babushka Tamara), who without a doubt made the best pirozhki ever.

Baba Toma's Pirozhki Dough

MAKES ABOUT 40 BUNS

—

1 teaspoon active-dry yeast

1 teaspoon sugar

3½ tablespoons warm water

generous 2 cups (500 ml)
    warm milk

1 egg yolk

1 egg white, lightly beaten

1 teaspoon salt

1 tablespoon vegetable oil,
    plus extra if frying the buns

6 cups (1 lb 10½ oz/750 g)
    all-purpose flour, plus
    extra for dusting

beaten egg, to glaze, if baking
    the buns

Mix the yeast, sugar, and warm water in a cup, then leave the mixture in a warm place for 5–10 minutes or until it starts to bubble.

In a large bowl, whisk together the warm milk, egg yolk, egg white, salt, oil, and activated yeast mixture until you get a smooth frothy liquid. Start adding the flour a cup at a time, whisking constantly to ensure there are no lumps. Once the whisk starts getting stuck in the dough, continue mixing with your hands. Eventually the dough should stop sticking to your hands. But if not, you can always add more flour at a later kneading stage. Once you have incorporated all the flour, cover the bowl with plastic wrap and let it rest for an hour or until it has doubled in size.

In the meantime, make your fillings (following the instructions in the next 3 recipes).

Once the dough has doubled in size, tip it out on to a generously floured work surface. Divide in half, then cover one half with a clean dish towel or plastic wrap while you knead the other. Work the dough for a few minutes, adding more flour as you go. If you don't want to make 40 buns at one time, the dough will keep, refrigerated, in a plastic food bag for up to 3 days, or it can be frozen.

Divide the dough into small chunks, 1½–1¾ oz (40–50 g) each, and pat them out as thinly as you can into 4 inch (10 cm) discs. Add 1–1½ tablespoons of filling to each disc and seal the edges by lifting them towards the middle and pressing together. Try to distribute the filling as evenly throughout as you can. Flatten each bun slightly, lay them out on a floured tray or sheet of parchment paper, and cover with plastic wrap while you finish the rest.

To cook the buns

The most difficult part is to decide whether you would like to opt for the indulgent pan-fried buns or the lighter oven-baked buns. I'll give you both methods here so that you can take your pick.

Heat about 3 tablespoons oil in a frying pan (the exact amount will depend on the size of your pan, of course, but this should be enough for a medium-sized one). Fry the buns for about 3 minutes on each side, if using a vegetable filling, and 5 minutes per side for a meat filling, until browned.

For baked buns, preheat the oven to 425°F (220°C). Place the buns on baking pans lined with parchment paper, brush with beaten egg, and bake for 30 minutes or until golden.

Belyashi Buns *with* Spiced Ground beef

FILLS 8–10 BUNS

—

14 oz (400 g) ground beef

1 onion, finely diced

4 garlic cloves, grated

2 teaspoons salt

2 teaspoons freshly ground
  black pepper

2 teaspoons coriander seeds,
  toasted and freshly ground
  (*see* page 31)

½ teaspoon red pepper flakes

2 tablespooons finely
  chopped dill

Belyashi is a traditional Tatar version of pirozhki, widely popular across the former Soviet Union. Distant cousins of samosas, these buns are shaped into triangles and the filling exposed through a little hole made in the middle.

To make the filling, simply mix the ground beef with all the other ingredients until evenly combined. To make the belyashi, place 1 tablespoon of the mixture in the middle of each dough disc. Pinch the edges of the dough together at the top and both sides to form a pyramid. Cook as instructed above.

Cabbage & Egg

Heat the oil in a large frying pan and fry the cabbage together with the scallions, dill, and some salt over low heat for 20 minutes, stirring occasionally. Add some water if the cabbage begins to catch. Once you are happy with the texture (it needs to retain a bit of crunch but also acquire a lovely caramelized quality), take off the heat and mix with the hard-boiled eggs. Adjust the seasoning to taste.

Cook as instructed on page 43.

FILLS 8–10 BUNS

—

2 tablespoons sunflower oil
¼ white cabbage, shredded
bunch of scallions,
    thinly sliced
bunch of dill, finely chopped
3 hard-boiled eggs, peeled
    and finely chopped
salt and freshly ground
    black pepper

Creamy Mushroom

Heat the oil in a frying pan and fry the mushrooms over medium heat for 5 minutes. Add the garlic and parsley to the pan, stir well and cook for a further 5 minutes. Take off the heat, drain off any excess liquid (mushrooms tend to release a lot of moisture when they cook) and stir through the sour cream. Season to taste.

Cook as instructed on page 43.

FILLS 8–10 BUNS

—

2 tablespoons sunflower oil
1 lb (500 g) cremini
    mushrooms, finely diced
2 garlic cloves, grated
4 tablespoons chopped flat-
    leaf parsley
3 tablespoons sour cream
salt and freshly ground
    black pepper

Herbs & Feta

Simply mix the feta with all the herbs and pepper until an even mixture is achieved.

Cook as instructed on page 43.

FILLS 8–10 BUNS

—

1⅔ cups (9 oz/250 g)
    crumbled feta cheese
6 tablespoons finely
    chopped dill
6 tablespoons finely chopped
    flat-leaf parsley
1 tablespoon finely chopped
    tarragon leaves
1 teaspoon freshly ground
    black pepper

Profiteroles *with* Chicken Liver Pâté

MAKES 20–25 SMALL BUNS

—

For the pâté

7 oz (200 g) chicken livers,
  sinew removed

1¼ cups (300 ml) milk

1 tablespoon (½ oz/15 g)
  unsalted butter

½ onion, finely diced

⅓ teaspoon ground nutmeg

½ teaspoon herbes de
  Provence

1 tablespoon brandy

1 tablespoon toasted pine nuts

salt and freshly ground
  black pepper

For the choux buns

scant 1 cup (3½ oz/100 g)
  all-purpose flour

pinch of salt

scant 1 cup (220 ml) water

6 tablespoons (3 oz/85 g)
  unsalted butter

3 eggs, at room temperature

Profiteroles were the absolute signature dish of my great-grandma Rosalia. Trained as a pastry chef, she really knew what she was doing when it came to baking and patisserie. While her repertoire was rather limited—invention and originality were not particularly on trend during the Soviet era—what she did make was so good that the entire family were happy to have it over and over again. Rosalia made both sweet and savory profiteroles using crème pâtissière and chicken liver pâté respectively, and below is her savory recipe, which has been adapted slightly by my mom. The pâté also works well on a piece of Melba toast with some chili jam if you don't feel like going to town and making the choux buns. Do give them a shot when you can, though, since they really are worth the trouble. This dish is a great way to make your guests swoon at the beginning of a party.

To make the pâté, first soak the chicken livers in the milk for 30 minutes, then drain them before using.

Melt the butter in a frying pan, add the chicken livers, and cook for 6 minutes, making sure there is no blood remaining. Then add the onion, nutmeg, and herbs and cook for 5 minutes until the onion has caramelized.

Transfer to a food processor and blend with the brandy and toasted pine nuts until smooth. You can then pass the pâté through a sieve to achieve an extra-silky consistency, if you like. Spoon into a pastry bag and refrigerate until needed.

To make the choux buns, preheat the oven to 425°F (220°C), and line a baking pan with parchment paper.

Sift the flour and salt onto another sheet of parchment paper.

Place the measured water and butter in a small saucepan and let the butter melt but don't let it boil. Once the butter has melted and the mixture is very hot, quickly tip the seasoned flour off the parchment paper into the pan and stir rapidly with a wooden spoon.

Take off the heat and continue beating the mixture until it forms a ball that comes away cleanly from the sides of the pan.

Beat the eggs in a bowl and then add little by little to the dough, mixing really well each time you add a batch before adding the next. This is a really physically demanding task, so don't despair—but maybe have someone spurring you on in the kitchen as you make the dough. You will know you have succeeded when the mixture becomes smooth and shiny and falls off the spoon easily.

Pipe or spoon small mounds of the dough on to the lined baking pan and bake for 20 minutes until well risen and golden brown. Turn the oven off and let the pastry cool completely in the oven—this is very important!

Make a small horizontal cut at the bottom of each bun and pipe in the pâté.

Serve to your guests and prepare to receive a standing ovation!

Deviled Eggs
with Forshmak

Another classic treat for a finger-food buffet or a canapés-style party. *Forshmak* (the Yiddish word for "foretaste") is a staple of Soviet-Jewish cuisine. While initially it was a term used to describe any cold appetizer made from finely chopped salty fish or meat, in Russian culture it is known as a pâté of salted herring, green apples, and onions. Light, creamy, and tangy, it is often served on a slice of rye bread or as a filling for deviled eggs. For me, forshmak is a word that I always associate with my great-grandma Rosalia. Pronounced with her heavy Ukrainian accent, this magical word was a source of endless silly giggles to me as a kid. I would ask her over and over again to say "forshmak," and like clockwork the giggles would follow. Even to this day, I sometimes forget its real definition and think it's my family's code word of sorts.

Place all the ingredients, apart from the cooked egg white halves but including the cooked egg yolks, in a food processor, making sure to squeeze out the excess milk from the bread, and process on high speed for 5–8 minutes until you get a smooth pâté. Taste for seasoning and acidity and adjust if needed, adding more salt, sugar, or lemon juice.

To make the deviled eggs, place the forshmak in a pastry bag fitted with a star tip (or with the corner snipped off) and pipe the mixture into the hollow of each egg white half.

Alternatively, you can serve forshmak as a pâté on a toasted slice of rye bread, in which case you don't need to remove the egg yolks from the whites. I love retro deviled eggs, so that would be my preferred way to serve forshmak at a dinner party.

SERVES 4–6

—

7 oz (200 g) salted herring fillets in oil (*see* page 235)

¼ white onion

1 Granny Smith apple, peeled and cored

½ oz (15 g) white bread, soaked in milk for 5 minutes and squeezed dry

finely grated zest and juice of 1 lemon, or more juice to taste

1 teaspoon salt, or more to taste

1 teaspoon sugar, or more to taste

generous pinch of freshly ground black pepper

1 tablespoon sunflower oil

1 tablespoon chopped dill

6 hard-boiled eggs, peeled, halved, and yolks carefully removed

rye bread toast, to serve (optional)

Stroganina Siberian Sashimi

Stroganina is one of the oldest ways of consuming freshwater whitefish in Siberia. Most common among indigenous Siberian people (Eskimo, Komi, and Yakut), these shavings of raw frozen whitefish have become an inseparable part of traditional Russian cuisine, dating back to pre-Soviet days. As pre-Revolutionary cuisine is enjoying a widespread revival today, dedicated stroganina "bars" have cropped up all over the country, competing with equally popular sushi restaurants. While it might seem odd to eat freshly caught fish frozen, you just have to trust this centuries-old tradition, since the sensation of the delicate fish melting in your mouth is unique. Traditionally, Siberian whitefish such as muksun and nelma are used for this dish, but you can make your own stroganina using their distant cousins char, trout, and salmon, as well as cod. Make sure to dress the fish generously with all the condiments, and have a shot of ice-cold vodka in hand!

Freeze your fish fillet immediately, unless your local fishmonger already has freshly caught frozen ones. Also place a serving tray in the freezer for 2 hours before you begin preparation.

When ready to serve, prepare all the condiments before the stroganina. Place them in individual little serving bowls to create an exciting gastronomic ceremony.

For the stroganina, remove the fish from the freezer and, using a very sharp knife or a vegetable peeler, cut the fillet, from the top, into long very thin strips, which will curl as you slice. Place on the frozen tray to keep ice-cold.

Serve the fish with the condiments immediately, before it starts to melt (this process should take place in your mouth and not sooner). Devour the same way as you would sashimi or oysters, and feel free to experiment with additional condiments, such as wasabi or a pungent mignonette (finely shopped shallot and freshly ground black pepper in red wine vinegar).

MAKES A STROGANINA
PLATTER FOR 4

—

14 oz (400 g) skinless frozen fish fillets of your choice, the freshest you can get

2 tablespoons sea salt flakes

2 tablespoons freshly ground black pepper

1 red onion, thinly sliced

scant ½ cup (100 ml) soy sauce

scant ½ cup (100 ml) rice vinegar or white wine vinegar (optional)

scant ½ cup (3½ oz/100 g) horseradish cream (*see* page 29)

1 lemon, cut into wedges (optional)

Winter Slaw

SERVES 4

—

½ red cabbage

1 red onion

1 red apple, cored

1 red pepper, cored and
  deseeded

2 generous handfuls of Red
  Sauerkraut with Garlic &
  Chili (*see* page 159), or
  store-bought sauerkraut

2 tablespoons dried sour
  cherries, plus extra to serve

bunch of dill

2 tablespoons sunflower
  seeds, toasted, plus extra
  to serve

finely grated zest and juice
  of 1 lemon

1 tablespoon red wine vinegar

2 tablespoons Red Sauerkraut
  with Garlic & Chili brining
  liquid (*see* page 159), or
  brine from your store-
  bought sauerkraut

2 pinches of sea salt flakes

pinch of sugar

1 garlic clove, grated (optional)

1 small hot red chili pepper,
  finely chopped (optional)

This recipe came about quite recently when I was planning on making a traditional Russian "Vitamin Salad," but then remembered I had some sauerkraut sitting in my refrigerator. And, as often happens, I fell down the rabbit hole of culinary improvisation. Adding a few new ingredients to the simple cabbage, red pepper, and carrot slaw, I ended up with a sharp and textural salad, far more complex in flavor than the Soviet prototype so popular in all kindergarten and school cafeterias.

You can use either white or red cabbage, depending on your mood and the season. The richly colored purple cabbage I use here is undoubtedly best suited to a cozy candlelit winter meal. What I love most about this salad is its versatility: replace the sauerkraut and sunflower seeds with pomegranate seeds and molasses and you have yourself a Middle Eastern-style slaw that will be a perfect accompaniment to any mezze spread.

This salad requires a whole lot of fine chopping, so if you have a mandolin, your task will be a lot faster and easier, albeit more dangerous to the well-being of your fingers (I speak from experience here, since I type this recipe with both thumbs out of action!).

Thinly slice the cabbage, onion, apple, and red pepper into a large mixing bowl. Add the sauerkraut and mix together well.

Finely chop the dried sour cherries and most of the dill (reserving some for topping the salad), then add to the bowl along with sunflower seeds.

To make the dressing, mix together the lemon zest and juice, vinegar, sauerkraut brine, sea salt, and sugar. If you are using the homemade sauerkraut from the book, then your salad will automatically get the kick of garlic and chili from it. If using any other sauerkraut, then add the garlic and chili pepper.

Pour the dressing over the salad and massage well for a few minutes to let all the flavors mingle.

Cover and keep in the refrigerator for a few hours before serving to get the maximum flavor.

Serve in a large bowl topped with the reserved dill and some extra dried sour cherries and toasted sunflower seeds.

Herring *in* Furs

—

1 raw red beet, washed

mild vegetable oil, for rubbing
  and dressing the beet

8–10 baby potatoes, scrubbed

8–10 baby carrots, scrubbed

2 eggs

4 teaspoons beet juice (*see*
  method to make your own),
  or more to taste

generous 1 cup (9 oz/250 g)
  crème fraîche

1 small garlic clove, grated

2 pinches of sea salt flakes

4 salted herring fillets in oil

small bunch of dill

good-quality unrefined
  sunflower oil, for drizzling

salt and freshly ground
  black pepper

I can bet you all the (little) money I have that anyone from the former Soviet Union reading this recipe will have a huge smile on their face and a sense of childlike excitement thinking of their favorite holiday—New Year's Eve. This dish is essentially synonymous with the feast on December 31st, since it is one of the several iconic appetizers to adorn the festive table, along with Russian salad (aka Olivier salad—*see* page 59) and meat in aspic, called *Kholodets* (*see* page 61). The furs of the title refer to a rich layer of boiled and grated beets, carrots, potatoes, and eggs, as well as of raw onions and mayo. The original name in Russian—*seledka pod shuboi*—translates as "herring under a fur coat." My title for the dish makes a playful nod to the famous literary *Venus in Furs*, since my herring's coat is a lot lighter and more elegant than the one worn by her Soviet ancestor.

Preheat the oven to 400°F (200°C). Rub the beet with a little oil and sprinkle with salt, then wrap in foil and roast for 30 minutes or until cooked but retaining a bit of crunch—pierce to the middle with a knife to check. Let the beet cool down, then peel and cut into 8 wedges. Dress with a bit of oil and salt and set aside.

Cook the baby potatoes and carrots in separate saucepans of salted boiling water for 10 minutes or until tender. Drain and cut the potatoes into halves or quarters, depending on their size, and the carrots in half lengthways.

Cook the eggs in boiling water for 8 minutes. I know I am stating the obvious here, but make sure to add the eggs only once the water is boiling, and then drain and run them under cold water afterwards to ensure they peel easily.

While the vegetables and eggs are cooking, make the dressing. To obtain a small shot of beet juice, you can either use a juicer, or finely grate a small raw beet and strain the pulp through a fine sieve. Stir it into the crème fraîche in a small bowl. The amount of juice you add to the crème fraîche is really up to you, depending on the color you prefer, but about 4 teaspoons will turn it the most delightful light pink color. Add the garlic and season with salt and pepper to taste—I usually add 2 pinches of sea salt flakes, which is less salty and iodine-tasting than standard table salt.

Once the vegetables and eggs are boiled, assemble the salad.

Place 2 dollops of the crème fraîche dressing on a large serving plate and spread it over evenly. Serve the rest in a bowl on the side. Cut the herring fillets into bite-sized slices and scatter around. Add the beet wedges, potatoes, and carrots, making sure you are not overcrowding the plate. Peel the eggs and cut into wedges, then place them on the plate, adding more texture and color to the composition.

The final touches to this dish are a light flourish of dill. Give it another grind of salt and pepper and a little drizzle of unrefined sunflower oil before serving.

Salt & Time

58

Olivier Salad

Known as Russian salad all over the world, this dish is the icon of Soviet gastronomy in general and of the New Year's Eve feast in particular. Replacing Christmas in the secular Soviet state, New Year's Eve became the key holiday, uniting us all in an identical ritual: preparing a feast of "salads" heavily laden with mayo while watching the archetypal New Year's Eve-themed film *The Irony of Fate*. While I haven't celebrated New Year's Eve in Russia for a very long time, every year on the December 31st, like clockwork, I long for that bizarre film–food ritual! Traditionally Olivier is made with mayo—it is the quintessential Soviet salad after all. However, if you would like to skip the heavy dressing, try my suggestion below.

I know this salad could work quite well as a meal on its own, but I can only imagine it served as part of a large festive spread of salads and dips.

The cooking method for this salad could not be simpler, yet also more time-consuming.

Peel and cook the potatoes and carrots in separate saucepans of lightly salted boiling water. Depending on their sizes, they will need 25–35 minutes. You can reuse the water to boil the eggs, which will need about 8 minutes, or boil them at the same time in another saucepan. Once their time is up, drain and run the eggs under cold water, then peel and set aside.

To defrost the peas, simply place them in a colander and pour some boiling water over them.

Once all the veggies and the eggs are cooked, dice the veggies along with the cucumbers as identically as you can and mix in a large bowl with the peas.

I prefer my salad vegetarian, but you can (as millions of Russians do) add the boiled chicken breast, diced to match the vegetables, to the mix.

To make the dressing, put all the ingredients in a bowl and give them a good stir, seasoning with salt and pepper to taste. Add the dressing to the salad ingredients and mix together thoroughly.

Divide the dressed salad among 4 plates. For a traditional presentation, dice the cooled, peeled egg and add it to the mix, or break with tradition and cut them in half and top each salad with an egg half before serving.

SERVES 4

—

For the salad
2 potatoes
2 carrots
2 eggs
1¾ cups (9 oz/250 g) frozen peas
2 pickled or Fermented Cucumbers (*see* page 152)
2 medium boneless, skinless chicken breasts, poached (optional)
salt

For the dressing
generous ¾ cup (7 oz/200 g) crème fraîche
generous ¾ cup (7 oz/200 g) Greek yogurt
small bunch of dill, finely chopped
juice of ½ lemon
salt and freshly ground black pepper

Kholodets

Completing the Holy Trinity of Soviet New Year's Eve appetizers is *kholodets*. This dish is achieved by chilling rich meat stock together with pulled beef until it turns into a jelly. However, no setting agents are added to this dish, since all you need to do is create the richest, clearest stock known to humankind. A bit of a laborious endeavor, it makes sense that kholodets was reserved for special occasions such as New Year's Eve. In my family, this important task always fell on the shoulders of my grandparents, who never failed to live up to our high standards. They would always appear on our doorstep on the evening of December 31st, their fur coats covered in snow, with a large white enamel tray in their hands. To this day, whenever I think of kholodets I immediately see that old-fashioned Soviet enamel tray. Traditionally this dish was made only in winter, back in the days when refrigerators were not an option and kholodets (from the Russian *kholod*, meaning "cold") would not have survived without very low temperatures. However, these days I would encourage you to prepare kholodets all year round, since it makes a delightful cool dish in spring or summer, too.

In a large stockpot, combine all the ingredients, but use only 1 carrot and 1 onion to begin with. Bring to a boil and skim off the foam, then reduce the heat to a simmer and cook, part-covered, for 12 hours. The trick to a clear stock is to change the onions and carrots every 3 hours, so as you discard the old batch, add a new one. You will know the stock is ready when you dip your finger into the pot and can feel a sticky consistency.

Remove the meat and discard all of the vegetables. Strain the broth through a sieve lined with 2 layers of paper towels. Strain 3 times, changing the paper towels each time, to catch all the fat and impurities. Pull the meat away from the bone and arrange in an even layer in the base of a rectangular baking dish. Top with the stock, and refrigerate overnight. Cross your fingers and go to bed! Your kholodets should be ready in the morning as it turns into a beautiful clear amber jelly.

Cut into 8–10 slices and serve with some rye bread, rubbed with garlic, and a good Eastern European mustard.

SERVES 8–10

—

4½ lb (2 kg) beef shin, on the bone

4 carrots, skin on

4 white onions, skin on

3 garlic cloves, skin on

2 bay leaves

bunch of flat-leaf parsley, leaves and stalks

1 tablespoon black peppercorns

2 tablespoons salt, or to taste

10½ cups (2.5 liters) water

To serve

rye bread rubbed with garlic

good Eastern European mustard

An Easter party:
Salmon and Caviar Blini Cake
(*see* page 106)
Easter Paskha Cake
(*see* page 176)
Blinis (*see* page 184)

Soups

Chapter 2

A renowned Russian food historian, William Pokhlebkin (whose pen name derives from the Russian word for "stew"), claimed that one could spot a happy family by the presence or absence of soups in their meals. My mom, aware of that opinion, prides herself on the fact that in her household there is always soup on any given day of the year. Soup does indeed offer a sense of comfort and togetherness, and also delights us in the anticipation of the main course, turning a meal into a ceremony. When I think of Russian broths and soups, I can immediately taste *smetana* as well as rye bread with butter. It is interesting how our food memory works; I think this association is very telling of the soup-eating culture that I grew up in. No matter the soup itself, you can never go wrong with a dollop of sour cream and a generously buttered slice of rye bread, so do bear that in mind when reading this chapter.

Sorrel & Cucumber
Botvinia

—

14 oz (400 g) bunch of sorrel

14 oz (400 g) mixed winter
   greens, such as chard,
   spinach, and beet greens

1 large cucumber, peeled
   and roughly chopped

2–3 garlic cloves, grated

4 hard-boiled eggs, peeled
   and halved

¼ cup (2 oz/60 g) sour cream
   or Greek yogurt

1½ cups (3½ oz/100 g) mixed
   soft herbs, such as tarragon,
   dill, and flat-leaf parsley,
   finely chopped

squeeze of lemon juice
   (optional)

salt

Botvinia is an old Russian soup made from leafy greens and beet greens and served cold in spring and summer. While the soup traditionally uses *kvass*—a Russian fermented bread drink—I've omitted it here to let the wonderful lemony tang of sorrel shine through. In my mind, sorrel and spring are synonymous. When I still lived in Russia, our family would enjoy an array of sorrel soups come spring, and its unique fresh flavor was a vibrant sign that the seasons had changed. Most soup recipes featuring sorrel also include boiled eggs, since there is something to be said about the union of the tanginess and creaminess of the two ingredients. Ever since I've lived abroad, the unique flavor of sorrel soup has become a distant memory. But fortunately, in recent years sorrel has begun to crop up at farmers' markets, and when I first saw it I could not believe my luck—that inimitable taste, which makes the mouth water, was back in my life!

Traditionally, botvinia is served with a side of cold poached salmon, so by all means add the fish to your meal, but I prefer this soup vegetarian.

Wash the sorrel and greens, then blanch, in batches, in a large pan of salted boiling water for 2 minutes. Have a bowl of cold water with ice cubes nearby, and as each batch is cooked, scoop it out of the pot with a sieve and transfer to the iced water for 30 seconds or so. Don't be alarmed when the sorrel turns dark as it hits the boiling water, since the color will be balanced out by the rest of the greens.

Once all the vegetables have cooled down, drain well and transfer to a food processor, together with the cucumber and garlic. Blend together into a smooth purée. The soup will have the consistency of a smoothie, so if you prefer yours a little runnier, then add a few tablespoons of cold water or a handful of ice cubes. Add 2 teaspoons of salt, give the soup another blend, and adjust the seasoning to taste.

To serve the soup, divide among 4 bowls, top each with 2 hard-boiled egg halves and a dollop of sour cream or yogurt, and generously sprinkle with the chopped herbs. Add some lemon juice, if you like, and more salt to taste.

Ukha
Rustic Fish Soup

To me, the beauty of *ukha* is that no matter where or when I eat it, I'm transported to a campfire, with a large cast-iron pot of this wonderful fish soup bubbling away. Since the soup is traditionally prepared outdoors on an open fire, it is characterized by a slightly smoky quality that you can imitate at home as I have suggested in the recipe below. Admittedly, it's unconventional, so feel free to omit it. While ukha is made with local fresh-water fish, I make this soup using salmon, which works equally well. Make sure to add an abundant amount of dill and freshly ground black pepper, and get ready to be lifted from your seat!

To make the delicious fish broth, place all the ingredients in a large stockpot and bring to a boil. Skim off any foam, then reduce the heat and simmer gently for 2 hours, topping up the water if it reduces too much. Taste the broth for seasoning and adjust as necessary.

Strain through a fine sieve or a cheesecloth, reserving the liquid and discarding the solids.

Bring the broth back to a boil in the pot, adding the finely sliced carrots, onion, and potato chunks, and cook for 7–10 minutes until the potatoes are soft.

Tip the shot of vodka into the soup (you can drink one yourself, too!). If you would like to add a smoky quality to the soup, light a wooden toothpick and extinguish it by dipping it into the broth.

Reduce the heat and add the salmon fillets. (You can leave them whole or roughly chop into medium-sized chunks.) Gently poach the salmon for no more than 5 minutes.

To serve, divide the salmon among 4 bowls, ladle in the broth, and generously sprinkle with the chopped dill and black pepper.

SERVES 4

—

For the fish broth

12⅔ cups (3 liters) water

1 large onion, skin on, halved

2 carrots, peeled and roughly chopped

2¼ lb (1 kg) fish bones, heads, and tails

3 bay leaves

1 tablespoon black peppercorns

2 generous pinches of sea salt flakes, plus extra to taste

For the soup

2 carrots, peeled and finely sliced into discs

1 onion, peeled and finely sliced

4 waxy potatoes, such as Yukon Gold, peeled and cut into bite-sized chunks

3½ tablespoons vodka

4 skinless salmon fillets (each 7 oz/200 g)

large bunch of dill, chopped

4 pinches of freshly ground black pepper

Borsch

SERVES 4

—

unrefined sunflower oil, for
    frying and roasting

1 large onion, finely diced

1 carrot, peeled and grated

6 raw red beets

2 red peppers

2 tablespoons tomato paste

8½ cups (2 liters) cold water

2 bay leaves

1 tablespoon black
    peppercorns

1 tablespoon coriander seeds

1 tablespoon fennel seeds

4 garlic cloves, peeled

bunch of dill

small bunch of flat-leaf parsley

2 garlic cloves, grated

1 lb (500 g) Red Sauerkraut
    with Garlic & Chili (*see*
    page 159)

2 tablespoons pomegranate
    molasses

1 red onion

1 tablespoon brown sugar

14 oz (400 g) can red kidney
    beans

2 teaspoons smoked paprika

4 tablespoons sour cream

salt

Borsch to Eastern Europe and Russia is like hummus to the Middle East. We all eat it, we all love it, yet we simply can't imagine that any other country owns the rights to it. It has its origin in a hogweed soup commonly consumed by the Slavs from the 15th to 16th centuries in territories occupied today by Poland, Ukraine, and Russia. There are so many variations of the soup, not only in each country, but in different regions within those countries, that borsch often becomes synonymous with Eastern European soup. As much as I love a good traditional borsch, and to me this means a passionately red beet soup cooked with a soffritto base as my Jewish–Ukrainian great-grandma would do, I sometimes struggle eating a plateful of chunky discolored vegetables that have given all their best to the broth. So here I am taking a bit (okay, a lot) of creative license, offering my own take on the iconic dish that consists of a rich red broth, raw sauerkraut, roasted vegetables, and baked red kidney beans. Lovers of traditional borsch recipes look away—this one is pretty iconoclastic!

If you can make the broth 24 hours in advance, you will be rewarded with an even better tasting soup, but a few hours of resting will also do the trick.

Heat up a tablespoon of sunflower oil in a large pot and fry the onion and carrot for about 8 minutes until golden. Meanwhile, peel and grate 2 of the beets, and core, deseed, and thinly slice 1 red pepper. Add the vegetables to the pot, together with the tomato paste and a splash of water. Season with salt to taste and fry for a further 5–8 minutes.

Top with the measured cold water, and add the bay leaves, peppercorns, all of the seeds, the whole garlic cloves, and half of the dill and parsley. Season with 1 tablespoon of salt and bring to a boil. Reduce the heat, add the grated garlic and half of the sauerkraut with its brine, and simmer, covered, over low heat for 40 minutes–1 hour.

Turn off the heat and let the borsch rest for another hour while you prepare the rest of the elements.

So far, so good, but here is where the recipe starts to deviate from the norm quite a lot: to prepare the vegetables that will grace the plate and also add extra flavor and texture to the soup, you will need to do a bit of roasting.

Start by preheating the oven to 350°F (180°C).

Peel the remaining 4 beets, cut them into wedges, and dress with oil, salt, and the pomegranate molasses. Peel the red onion, cut it into wedges, and season with salt and the brown sugar to bring out their sweetness and promote caramelization. Place the beets and onions on a roasting pan and roast together for 30 minutes. Drain the kidney beans, then dress them with salt, oil, and the smoked paprika. Core and deseed the remaining red pepper, then cut into thin strips and dress with salt and oil. Roast the beans and pepper together, since they will need only 10–15 minutes.

When ready to serve, strain the broth through a sieve or cheesecloth, discarding the solids. All we need is that rich broth! Reheat if necessary. Next, create layers of texture and flavor in each bowl by adding a heaped tablespoon of the remaining sauerkraut to each, as well as a handful of roasted beet, onion, kidney beans, and red pepper. Top each bowl with the hot broth and add a dollop of sour cream and a generous sprinkle of the remaining dill and parsley (chopped). The intensity of the flavors and textures of this dish is beyond words, while the look of the bowl will seduce the eye without a doubt.

Okroshka

SERVES 4

—

1 large cucumber

4 hard-boiled eggs, peeled

10 radishes

bunch of dill

bunch of flat-leaf parsley

bunch of chives

1¼ cups (7 oz/200 g) drained
   canned or cooked chickpeas

3⅓ cups (800 ml) Kvass (see
   page 222), Iranian doogh, or
   Turkish ayran

4 tablespoons sour cream
   (if using kvass)

4 teaspoons horseradish
   cream (see page 29) or
   Eastern European mustard

salt and freshly ground
   black pepper

If you say "okroshka" to me, I immediately see a bright summer day, since this herbaceous tangy cold soup is nothing short of a sunny meadow in a bowl. Another example of a pre-Revolutionary recipe that was simplified and popularized during the Soviet era, okroshka, as its name suggests (from the Russian kroshit, meaning "to crumble or finely chop"), is a mixture of finely diced vegetables, cold meats, and soft herbs, topped with the sparkling fermented bread drink, kvass, and sour cream. Preferring my soup vegetarian, I exclude the meat but double the herbs and, rather unconventionally, throw in some chickpeas to add a bit of that "meaty" texture. When making this dish abroad, where I don't always have homemade kvass on hand, I resort to Iranian doogh or Turkish ayran, salty pouring yogurts. Some horseradish cream or Eastern European mustard adds an extra kick!

This works so well as a light lunch (in which case you are likely to have seconds) or as a very refreshing appetizer for a summer feast.

Finely dice the cucumber, eggs, and radishes.

Chop all the herbs and put them in a large mixing bowl, together with the eggs, vegetables, and chickpeas. Season with salt and black pepper to taste.

Divide the mixture equally between 4 bowls, top each with generous ¾ cup (200 ml) kvass, doogh, or ayran, and add a dollop of sour cream (if using kvass), as well as a teaspoon of horseradish cream or mustard.

Svekolnik

SERVES 4

—

3 large raw red beets
   with leaves

3 garlic cloves, grated

1 onion, peeled and halved

1 carrot, peeled and cut
   into chunks

1 tablespoon black
   peppercorns

1 tablespoon salt

1 tablespoon apple
   cider vinegar

6⅓ cups (1.5 liters) water

For the toppings

1 boiled potato, diced

1 cucumber, peeled and diced

4 radishes, diced

1 hard-boiled egg, peeled
   and diced

½ cup (1 oz/30 g) mixed fresh
   herbs, such as dill, flat leaf
   parsley, and chives

4 tablespoons horseradish
   cream (*see* page 29)

Back in my film-scholar days, I had an ultimate dream-come-true moment when I attended a festival celebrating my favorite film director, Andrei Tarkovsky. Taking place in a beautiful pastoral setting on the banks of the River Volga, the festival was not only an incredible artistic experience but also a very memorable gastronomic one. Serving classics of Russian cuisine, the local restaurants treated us to some of the best dishes I've ever had, one of them being a simple *svekolnik* soup, which I remember (and crave) to this day. Svekolnik is pretty much a cold *borsch*. But whereas there are myriad ways and ingredients with which borsch can be prepared, there is no debate about the key ingredient of svekolnik: well, it's *svekla*, the Russian word for "beet." Deep in color and wonderfully earthy in flavor, it's served with a topping of cold vegetables and fresh herbs, along with a giant dollop of horseradish cream.

Make sure to select the freshest beets available: the leaves will be great indicators of that.

Peel the beets, cut into wedges, and roughly chop the leaves and stalks. Place in a large pot with the rest of the ingredients. Bring to a boil, then simmer, covered, over medium heat for 40 minutes.

Turn off the heat and let it cool and infuse at room temperature. Then transfer to a bowl, cover, and refrigerate for a few hours.

Strain the soup using a fine sieve; you might want to use cheesecloth, too, to catch any fine particles and make sure you get the clearest broth possible.

Serve cold with all the toppings, and don't be shy with the horseradish cream!

A Mushroom Broth *with* an Asian Touch

We all know that chicken broth is a cure-all dish. Common in most Eastern European countries, and hence in Ashkenazi cuisine as well, it's often lovingly referred to as Jewish penicillin. While I have been raised on the loveliest "penicillin" thanks to my Jewish great-grandma, when I moved away from home, my preferred cure-all dish became a simple mushroom broth. Made with an assortment of mushrooms and a soffritto of onion and carrot, this rich broth could not be simpler to prepare and is guaranteed to make you feel healthier by the spoonful.

While this soup is quintessentially Eastern European, I've recently discovered that an addition of soy sauce and soba noodles turns it into a hearty affair with an East Asian flavor. What's more, if you top each bowl with a generous dollop of *Khrenovina* (*see* page 158) you will get yourself nothing short of a miraculous elixir!

Soak the wild mushrooms in the measured boiling water for 10–15 minutes.

In the meantime, heat the oil in a medium pot and fry the onion and carrot over medium heat for 5–8 minutes until softened.

Drain the wild mushrooms, reserving the liquid for later, and add to the pot, along with the cremini mushrooms, garlic, and parsley. Season with the salt and cook for a further 5 minutes.

Pour in the vegetable stock and mushroom soaking liquid, as well as the soy sauce, and bring to a boil. Reduce the heat and simmer, covered, for 30 minutes.

To serve, cook the soba noodles according to the package instructions. Drain and divide the cooked noodles among 6 bowls, top with the hot mushroom broth and add a tablespoon of khrenovina and a sprinkle of parsley to each serving. I am already feeling better just thinking about this dish!

SERVES 6

—

For the mushroom broth

¾ oz (20 g) dried wild mushrooms

scant ½ cup (100 ml) boiling water

1 tablespoon mild vegetable oil

1 onion, diced

1 carrot, peeled and grated

1 lb (500 g) cremini mushrooms, sliced

2 garlic cloves, grated

bunch of flat-leaf parsley, leaves and stalks finely chopped

1 teaspoon salt

8½ cups (2 liters) vegetable stock

2 tablespoons soy sauce

To serve

10½ oz (300 g) soba noodles

6 tablespoons Khrenovina (*see* page 158)

¼ cup (½ oz/15 g) finely chopped flat-leaf parsley

Potato & Caviar Soup

SERVES 4

—

2 tablespoons (1 oz/30 g)
  unsalted butter

1 small onion, diced

2 garlic cloves, grated

2 leeks, white parts only,
  thinly sliced

small bunch of dill leaves and
  stalks, chopped, plus
    extra to garnish

small bunch of flat-leaf
  parsley, leaves and stalks

8–10 potatoes, peeled and
  roughly diced

6⅓ cups (1.5 liters) vegetable
  stock

2 bay leaves

¼ cup (60 ml) heavy cream

4 teaspoons salmon caviar

salt and freshly ground
  black pepper

toasted rye bread with butter,
  to serve

At first sight, this recipe might appear to feed into the glamorous stereotype of rich Russians consuming caviar by the ladleful with every meal. However, back in Soviet days, when the presence of caviar on one's table was indeed a true sign of privilege, this sought-after delicacy was actually commonplace in a few regions of the vast country. I was really surprised to find out that my dad, who comes from a humble family of Soviet geologists, grew up on a diet of potatoes and caviar. Spending his youth on geological expeditions with his parents in the Russian Far East, he had no choice but to eat freshly caught local fish, and its caviar. What a dream!

While the original dish of mashed potatoes and quick-cured caviar did not seem to cut it for a cookbook, I was pleasantly surprised to discover that my food stylist Tamara Vos, who shares a name with my paternal grandma, has improvised on the theme of Russian cuisine, creating her own recipe for a potato and caviar soup. What an incredible and uncanny coincidence!

Melt the butter in a medium pot and fry the onion, garlic, leeks, and herbs over low heat for 10–15 minutes. Add the potatoes and cover with the vegetable stock, then stir in the bay leaves and season with salt and pepper to taste. Bring to a boil, then reduce the heat and simmer the soup for 20–30 minutes until the potatoes are cooked and tender.

Remove from the heat, remove the bay leaves, and add the heavy cream. Whizz with a handheld immersion blender until you have a smooth, silky consistency without any lumps. Taste for seasoning and adjust if necessary.

Pour the soup into bowls and garnish each with a teaspoon of caviar and some extra dill. I know I keep advising to serve rye toast with the soups, but it is here that a generously buttered warm slice of Russian rye bread definitely *must* be had.

Shchi

—

1 tablespoon sunflower oil

½ onion, thinly sliced

1 carrot, peeled and grated

2 cups (7 oz/200 g) cremini
    mushrooms, roughly
    chopped

9 oz (250 g) sauerkraut in
    brine

5½ cups (1.3 liters) vegetable
    stock

4 bay leaves

4 potatoes, peeled and cubed

handful of dill, finely chopped

salt and freshly ground
    black pepper

sour cream, to garnish

This rather unpronounceable soup is believed to be the most popular dish in Russia, spanning Tsarist, Soviet, and post-Soviet times. Consisting of a few basic ingredients—cabbage or sauerkraut, onion, carrots, and potatoes—it somehow manages to taste complex and rich. While it is usually made with beef, I love this vegetarian version of *shchi* with mushrooms. Though it's a perfect soup for fall or winter, it works equally well in the summer, consumed at room temperature. And, like any soup that contains fermented vegetables, the good old *shchi* has rescued me from a bad hangover on more than one occasion. Make a big batch and keep in the refrigerator for up to 4 days. It will taste even better each time.

Heat the oil in a medium stockpot and fry the onion and carrot with a teaspoon of salt over medium heat for 5 minutes. Once the onion has softened, add the mushrooms and sauerkraut and cook for a further 5 minutes.

Next, add the vegetable stock, bay leaves, and another small pinch of salt. Cover the pot and bring to a boil. Then reduce the heat and simmer for 30 minutes.

Add the potato cubes to the pot and cook for a further 15 minutes. Turn off the heat and let the soup rest for 20–30 minutes. To me this is the most difficult part of the recipe—oh, the wait!

Serve hot with freshly ground black pepper and a dollop of sour cream, along with a slice of rye bread (of course).

Lagman

Omsk's proximity to Central Asia has always brought the advantage of culinary cross-pollination. Before Uzbek, Kazakh, and Tadzjik eateries became trendy all over Russia, Omsk inhabitants could enjoy the rich offerings of Central Asian cuisine at the simplest cafes. One of these was an Uzbek spot called "Kushon," occupying the oddly cozy space of an abandoned railway carriage behind one of the city's main markets. Besides serving the most delicious *lagman* soup, this place has a special significance in our family history, since it was the (rather unorthodox) venue for the celebration of my parents' 20th and 25th wedding anniversaries. So here is a recipe loosely based on the one served in the wonderfully trashy eatery that hosted the most festive celebrations in our family's history.

Heat the oil in a large saucepan and brown the beef over high heat for 10 minutes. Reduce the heat to medium, then add the onion and green peppers and fry for 5 minutes until the vegetables have softened.

Add the rest of the ingredients in the list up to (but not including) the measured water, give them a good stir, and cook for a few minutes.

Next, add the water with the bay leaves, cinnamon, and star anise. Bring to a boil, then reduce the heat and cook over medium heat for an hour or until the meat is really tender.

Turn off the heat, add the fresh herbs and vinegar, and let the ingredients infuse for 10–15 minutes.

In the meantime, cook the noodles according to the package instructions and get your extra herbs and chili ready for the table for your diners to dig in, DIY style.

Drain and divide the cooked noodles among 4 bowls, top with the soup, making sure you get as many chunky veggies and meat in there as possible, and serve immediately. Encourage your diners not to be shy with the herbs and chili!

SERVES 4

—

2 tablespoons mild vegetable oil

7 oz (200 g) diced beef chuck

1 onion, thinly sliced

2 green peppers, cored, deseeded, and thinly sliced

1 carrot, peeled and diced

½ daikon radish, peeled and diced

2 large garlic cloves, grated

2 tablespoons tomato paste

2 teaspoons sugar

2 teaspoons salt

2 teaspoons toasted and ground coriander seeds

2 teaspoons toasted and freshly ground cumin seeds

1 teaspoon red pepper flakes

1 teaspoon smoked paprika

1 teaspoon toasted and freshly ground allspice berries

6⅓ cups (1.5 liters) water

4 bay leaves

1 cinnamon stick

2 star anise

4 tablespoons chopped mixed dill and flat-leaf parsley, plus extra to garnish

1 tablespoon malt vinegar or distilled white vinegar

4 nests of dried egg or rice noodles

To serve
mint leaves
cilantro
fresh chili pepper, sliced

Goroshnitsa
Pea Soup

SERVES 4

—

1½ cups (10½ oz/300 g) dried
    yellow split peas

8½ cups (2 liters) water

2 vegetable or pork bouillon
    cubes

2 bay leaves

7 oz (200 g) pancetta, diced

7 oz (200 g) smoked pork
    sausage, diced

4 smoked pork ribs, whole, on
    the bone

1 onion, finely diced

1 large carrot, peeled and
    grated

freshly ground black pepper

As a huge fan of spicy Turkish red lentil soup, I was delighted to remember that my native Russian cuisine has something similar: a yellow split pea soup with smoked meat called *goroshnitsa*. A perfect fall and winter comfort dish, the soup is a great way to use up any leftover smoked meats and sausages you might have in the refrigerator. But of course, by all means do purchase the loveliest smoked pork ribs and other fatty delights such as pancetta and cured lardo specifically for the occasion. Writing this recipe, I also remembered that it was a favorite dish of my late grandpa Yuri. Both my mom and my granny always made a mean split pea soup, much to Yuri's delight. Sadly, he never had the chance to try mine, but something tells me that my version would have topped the charts.

Thoroughly rinse the yellow split peas under cold running water. Place in a large pot and add the measured water, along with the crumbled bouillon cubes and bay leaves. Cook, uncovered, over medium-high heat for about 40 minutes.

In the meantime, prepare the most fragrant soffritto. Heat a frying pan, add all the meats—they should start sizzling straight away, giving off a wonderfully smoky rich aroma—and fry over medium heat for 10–15 minutes, stirring occasionally. Then add the onion and carrot and fry for a further 8 minutes. The fat from the meat should be enough, but if the mixture starts to dry up and stick to the pan, add little bit of stock from the split peas.

Empty the frying pan into the soup pot with the boiling peas. Make sure to rinse the pan out with some of the pea stock so that you don't lose even the tiniest bit of the fragrant fatty soffritto. Generously season with black pepper and simmer over low heat for 20 minutes.

Taste for seasoning—I find the meat and the stock salty enough, so I have omitted extra salt here, but feel free to add it to your liking.

Portion out the soup into 4 bowls, making sure each diner gets a piece of rib, and dig in without further ado.

My Mom's *Chinese Soup*

SERVES 6

—

For the chicken broth

8½ cups (2 liters) water, plus extra when needed

1 tablespoon black peppercorns

1 tablespoon salt

3 bay leaves

2 onions, skin on and washed

2 carrots, skin on and washed

3 celery sticks

4 garlic cloves, skin on and washed

small bunch of parsley stalks

3 chicken legs

For the soup

6 tablespoons soy sauce, plus extra to serve

1 lb (500 g) Napa cabbage, shredded

4 garlic cloves, grated

3 nests of dried egg noodles

white sesame seeds, to garnish

For the quick-pickle garnish

½ cucumber

1 small carrot, peeled

handful of dill, chopped

4 tablespoons white wine vinegar

2 tablespoons sesame oil

1 tablespoon brown sugar

1 garlic clove, grated

It's been a while since I've eaten my mom's signature soup, but its flavor comes back to me as soon as I think of our old family kitchen in Omsk. It is the combination of fresh garlic, soy sauce, and napa cabbage that gives the soup its distinct, sweet and pungent taste, while a nice fatty chicken adds all the necessary nutritional value for enduring a long cold winter. The reason for the creation of this soup is wonderfully banal: a refrigerator forage during a hangover. But as with any other soup created for that purpose, it also works wonders to cure many other maladies, from a common cold to homesickness. Feel free to adjust the amount of garlic and soy sauce to your own taste, or better yet, equip your companions with a DIY kit of fresh garlic and soy sauce so that each can enhance their own bowl of steaming goodness to their liking. Having treated myself and my friends to this perfectly simple soup during a recipe-testing session recently, I felt that it would benefit from the addition of some Asian-style pickled vegetables, which give an extra kick.

To make a rich chicken broth, add all the broth ingredients to a large stockpot and bring to a boil, then simmer, part-covered, for any time between 4 and 8 hours (the longer the better, of course), adding extra water when necessary, since a lot will evaporate during the cooking.

While the broth finishes cooking, make the quick-pickle garnish. Julienne the cucumber and carrot, place in a non-reactive bowl and mix in the dill. Make the pickling brine by mixing together the vinegar, oil, sugar, and garlic—you may need to heat the mixture up in a small pan to help the sugar dissolve. Cool it down and pour over the vegetables. Give it a good stir, let it rest for 30 minutes at room temperature, and your quick-pickled garnish is ready!

Test your chicken: if the skin and meat come away from the bone very easily, it is ready. It's essential to make sure that the chicken is cooked to its perfect, melt-in-your-mouth state. Separate the chicken meat from the skin and bones (discard these), and set aside. Strain the broth through a sieve to extract a pure stock that should be rich and golden in color.

Return the broth to the pot, together with the chicken meat. Add the soy sauce, Napa cabbage, and garlic, and bring back to a boil. Make sure to turn off the heat straightaway, since you don't want the napa cabbage to overcook. Let the soup rest, covered, to infuse while you cook the noodles according to the package instructions.

Drain and divide the cooked noodles among soup bowls (I serve only half a portion per person so that the noodles don't overpower the flavor of the soup or dominate the bowl visually). Pour over the soup and sprinkle with sesame seeds to garnish. Keep a plate of quick pickles close by!

Solyanka Fish Soup

SERVES 4

—

For the fish stock (optional)

1 lb (500 g) fish bones, heads, and skins (ask your fishmonger for the best assortment)

1 onion, skin on, halved

1 carrot, peeled and roughly chopped

4 bay leaves

dill and flat-leaf parsley stalks

1 tablespoon black peppercorns

1 tablespoon allspice berries

1 tablespoon salt

8½ cups (2 liters) water (it will reduce during cooking)

For the soup

2 tablespoons sunflower oil

½ onion, diced

1 carrot, peeled and grated

2 tablespoons tomato paste

1 teaspoon smoked paprika (optional, if you don't have any hot-smoked fish)

2 salt-brined pickles, diced

6⅓ cups (1.5 liters) fish stock (from the recipe above, or you can use ready-made)

2 potatoes, peeled and cubed

generous 1 cup (5½ oz/150 g) pitted green olives, quartered

1 tablespoon capers in brine

Solyanka is one of the oldest Russian soups, and has its first mention in the iconic *Domostroi* book—a sort of a household bible published under Ivan the Terrible in 1547 that gave guidance on how to manage a good Christian home. Since solyanka is characterized by a rich broth, an abundance of spices, and a powerful tang of brined vegetables, it's astonishing to think today that this soup was initially looked down upon by the upper classes as a food of the simple people (hence a variation of the dish's name being *selyanka*, a derivative of the Russian word for "village"). Over the years, new ingredients were added to the soup to strengthen that inimitable tangy flavor, including lemons, olives, and capers, and for a very long time now, solyanka has been enjoyed widely by all. Traditionally it is made with either meat, fish, or mushrooms, but the richness of the stock and its brininess remain the trademark of all three versions. I prefer fish solyanka, since hot-smoked trout or salmon add something utterly magical to the soup.

If you are choosing to go the extra mile and make your own stock, here's what you do: In a medium stockpot, combine the fish parts, onion, carrot, bay leaves, dill and parsley stalks, all the spices, and the salt. Add the water and bring to a boil, then reduce the heat and simmer, uncovered, for about 1½ hours. Once you are happy with the flavor, strain the broth through a sieve or cheesecloth. You are now ready to make the tastiest solyanka.

Heat the oil in a medium-sized pot and fry the onion and carrot with a small pinch of salt over medium heat for 3–5 minutes. Add the tomato paste with a splash of the fish broth, the smoked paprika, if using, and pickles, and fry for a further 5 minutes.

Pour in the measured hot fish stock and bring to a boil. Add the potato cubes and cook for about 30 minutes. Add the olives, and then add the capers and pickled peppers, with 2 tablespoons of their brine each. Finish cooking everything together for another 15 minutes or so.

Cut the fresh salmon and hot-smoked trout or salmon into bite-sized chunks and add to the soup, followed by the lemon juice and slices and the herbs. Reduce the heat to the minimum and cook the fish for 5 minutes or until it is gently poached. Make sure not to overcook it. Taste for seasoning and adjust if necessary.

1 tablespoon sliced green
    pickled jalapeños or Turkish
    hot peppers in brine (if you
    like an extra kick)
9 oz (250 g) skinless fresh
    salmon fillet
7 oz (200 g) skinless hot
    smoked trout or salmon fillet
1 lemon, juice of ½,
    ½ thinly sliced
large bunch dill, finely
    chopped, plus extra to
    garnish
large bunch flat-leaf parsley,
    finely chopped, plus extra to
    garnish
salt and freshly ground
    black pepper

Serve very hot, garnished with an extra sprinkle of fresh herbs. You know you will be doing yourself some good by adding a generous chunk of fresh crunchy bread on the side (and maybe just one shot of ice-cold vodka?).

Rassolnik

Fermentation lies at the heart of Russian cuisine as one of the most ancient techniques of preparing food. As you will notice throughout this book, numerous recipes rely on sauerkrauts, *kvass,* or *rassol* (the fermentation liquid) for their distinct tangy flavor. This soup, which carries the name *rassol* in its very title, is the embodiment of such a tradition. While historically *rassolnik* is an old Russian dish, the go-to recipe in our family comes from Poland. Back in the 1970s, my mom took part in a school program that allowed Soviet kids to find pen pals in neighboring socialist countries. She hit the jackpot, since she was linked up with a boy in Poland (the most coveted country of all friendly socialist ones). After a few years of correspondence, my mom and her parents were invited—and most importantly permitted by the Soviet officials—to visit her pen pal. Along with a bag full of trendy garments, chewing gum, and fancy stationery, which made her the coolest teenager in school, she brought back this recipe for a good old Russian rassolnik, cooked by her Polish friend's mom. The delicious soup always reminds me of the interwoven nature of the Soviet and Slavic histories and cuisines.

To make the stock, place the brisket in a large pot with all the vegetables, spices, and salt, pour over the measured water, and bring to a boil, then cook over medium-high heat for 1 hour.

Lift the meat out and reserve, then strain the stock through cheesecloth. Cut the meat into bite-sized chunks and return to the pot with the strained stock. Bring back to a boil, add the pearl barley, and leave to cook for about 30 minutes. Then add the diced potatoes and cook for a further 15 minutes until tender.

Meanwhile, prepare the soffritto. Heat the oil in a frying pan and fry the onion and carrot over medium heat for 5 minutes. Then add the tomato paste, a splash of water, and the sugar, chili sauce, and pickles, and fry everything together for another 5–8 minutes.

Once the barley and the potatoes are cooked, tip the contents of the frying pan into the soup pot, stir, and cook together for 10 minutes. Add the crazy amount of sour cream, stir, and then, as soon as the soup starts to boil, take it off the heat. Add the parsley and serve immediately.

SERVES 4

—

For the stock
10½ oz (300 g) beef brisket
1 onion, skin on, halved
1 carrot, peeled
1 tablespoon black
    peppercorns
1 tablespoon allspice berries
1 tablespoons salt
8½ cups (2 liters) water

For the soup
¾ cup (5½ oz/150 g) pearl
    barley
2 large potatoes, peeled and
    diced
2 tablespoons sunflower oil
1 onion, finely diced
1 carrot, peeled and grated
2 tablespoons tomato paste
1 teaspoon sugar
1 teaspoon chili sauce of your
    choice
2 large salt-brined pickles,
    grated
1 cup (9 oz/250 g) sour cream
small bunch of flat-leaf parsley
    leaves, finely chopped

A summer party:
Buckwheat Vinegret Salad
(*see* page 34)
Semolina Cake (*see* page 178)
Sea Buckthorn Mors
(*see* page 225)
Fermented Cucumbers
(*see* page 152)
Okroshka (*see* page 74)

Main Dishes

Russian food, like Eastern European food in general, is commonly believed to be filling, bland, and grey, heavy with meat and potatoes. Luckily, in recent years there has been a renewed interest in the foods of these regions and perceptions have begun to shift. So I feel it is about time to take a fresh look at a huge range of dishes traditionally consumed as main courses in Russia. In this chapter I'd like to challenge the stereotype of "boring" Russian dishes and also to demonstrate the sheer variety of recipes that range far beyond the borders of Eastern European cuisine. In this chapter you will find some meat and potato combos, but—trust me—even the simplest dishes can be elevated with the addition of herbs and spices or by taking away one thing (as good old Coco Chanel taught us) to lighten things up a bit. On the following pages, I explore traditional grains popular around Russia, as well as plants specific to certain regions, sharing an array of recipes from stews and dumplings to pies and slow-cooked rice dishes.

Crayfish & Spinach
Savory Rice Pudding

A dish so decadent and rich that it could only belong to the pre-Soviet era of Russian culinary history. I came across this main course when delving into a classic cookbook of the Tsarist era, written by Elena Molokhovets in 1861. While I struggled to understand the exact method (my Imperial-era Russian is a bit rusty), the name alone immediately evoked a beautifully simple and delicate dish, as well as bringing to mind the creamy taste of rice pudding and spinach. So this recipe is a result of my guesswork and culinary improvisation, which led to a rather delicious crossbreed between risotto and rice pudding. This is the perfect dish for a Sunday lunch in spring and would taste even better accompanied by some chilled white wine.

Melt the butter in a medium saucepan and cook the onion, celery, and garlic over medium heat for 8–10 minutes until they become soft and translucent but not caramelized.

Next, add all the rice and stir for a minute or so, allowing it to absorb the butter. Pour in the stock and cook, uncovered, over medium heat for 30 minutes, stirring occasionally. If the stock you are using is already sufficiently seasoned, there is no need to add salt, but otherwise adjust the seasoning to taste.

Add the milk and cream, stir, and cook for a further 10 minutes over low heat.

Finally, add the crayfish tails and spinach, season with salt and pepper to taste, and dress with the lemon zest and juice. Turn off the heat, mix thoroughly, and leave to rest under a lid for 5 minutes before serving.

This dish looks so vibrant and delicate on a pared back, plain white plate that I would encourage you to opt for an elegantly understated piece of dinnerware.

SERVES 4

—

2 tablespoons (1 oz/30 g) unsalted butter

½ onion, diced

1 celery stick, thinly sliced

1 garlic clove, grated

½ cup (3½ oz/100 g) short-grain rice

generous 2 cups (500 ml) vegetable stock

⅔ cup (150 ml) milk

3 tablespoons heavy cream

9 oz (250 g) cooked peeled crayfish tails

6½ cups (7 oz/200 g) spinach, chopped

finely grated zest and juice of ¼ lemon

salt and freshly ground black pepper

Pan-fried Cod *with* Marinated Vegetables

SERVES 4

—

4 cod fillets, skin on, from
    a sustainable source
1 tablespoon sunflower oil
sea salt flakes
good-quality unrefined
    sunflower oil, to serve

For the marinated vegetables
½ cup (120 ml) apple cider
    vinegar
5 tablespoons water
2 tablespoons sugar
1 tablespoon salt
1 small garlic clove, grated
2 carrots
½ red pepper
¼ white onion

For the vegetable purée
2 tablespoons sunflower oil
1 onion, roughly chopped
1 red pepper, cored, deseeded,
    and roughly chopped
1 carrot, peeled and grated
sea salt
2 tablespoons tomato paste
¼ cup (60 ml) water
2 tablespoons chopped dill,
    plus extra sprigs to garnish
pinch of red pepper flakes
1 teaspoon white wine vinegar

A staple of Soviet cuisine, this dish tastes a lot better than it looks. I have always been a fan of cod smothered in a lightly pickled soffritto of carrots, onions, and peppers, but its rather sloppy appearance never made me want to serve this dish at a dinner party. And then one evening, on a lovely dinner date with my partner in Cape Town, I hit the culinary jackpot when the most gorgeous plate of cod and carrot cooked three ways landed on my table. There it was, the good old Soviet "fish under a marinade," only it had undergone a much-needed makeover. I could not wait to get back to my kitchen to test this new version! The final result left me very pleased: I could finally share my favorite "ugly" dish in a new and rather dashing guise.

First, let's pickle the vegetables. To make the marinade, mix together the vinegar, measured water, sugar, salt, and garlic in a large non-reactive bowl. Give the mixture a good whisk with a fork to dissolve the sugar and salt a little. Peel the carrots and cut into ribbons with a vegetable peeler. Core and deseed the red pepper and peel the onion, then thinly slice both. Place all the vegetables in the bowl with the pickling mixture and stir to coat. Leave in the refrigerator for 30 minutes–1 hour.

Next, we will make the vegetable purée, upon which our crispy fried cod will rest. Heat the oil in a pan and fry the onion, red pepper, and carrot with a pinch of salt over medium heat for 5 minutes. Add the tomato paste, measured water, dill, and red pepper flakes and fry for a further 5 minutes. Taste for seasoning and adjust if necessary. Transfer to a food processor, add the vinegar, and blend until you have a smooth purée. Set aside and keep warm.

Finally, pan-fry the cod to perfection: Pat the cod fillets dry with paper towels and add some sea salt to taste. Let them rest at room temperature for about 20 minutes, then pat dry again. Heat the oil in a nonstick frying pan and, when it is very hot but not smoking, add the cod fillets skin-side down. Season with sea salt and fry without disturbing for 4–5 minutes. Carefully turn the fillets over and fry for a further 2–3 minutes. You will see how the flesh will change its color from translucent to solid white. Season the crispy skin with more sea salt and transfer to paper towels while you prepare your serving plates.

To dish up, place 2 tablespoons of the vegetable purée in the middle of each plate. Then proudly place the perfect cod on top and garnish with a handful of marinated vegetables, making sure you drain the excess pickling juice before adding them to the plate. Drizzle with some good-quality sunflower oil, and drop over a few sprigs of dill to add a touch of green.

Spring Fishcakes

MAKES 8–10
—

⅓ white cabbage

3–4 scallions, finely sliced

bunch of dill, chopped

1 carrot, peeled and grated

½ tablespoon salt

9 oz (250 g) skinless cod loin
    from a sustainable source

2 eggs, lightly beaten

¼ cup (1 oz/30 g) cornstarch

zest and juice of 1 lemon

sunflower oil, for shallow-
    frying

pinch of sea salt flakes

This recipe came to me almost immediately when I was jotting down ideas for dishes for this chapter. Convinced that I had enjoyed these fishcakes when I still lived in Russia, I asked my mom and granny for our family recipe. Turns out they had never heard of the dish. Yet I could easily recall the wonderfully juicy, tender, and crunchy texture of the fishcakes. Having no idea where I got the memory from, I searched the Russian internet for clues. My research didn't return any satisfying results, instead releasing myriad different fishcake recipes, some called "Monastery Fishcakes," while others bearing the more appropriate name of "Tenderness." Taking the best from all versions, I've conjured up my own recipe, which, when tested, succeeded in bringing back that wonderful flavor and texture that I mysteriously remember so well.

This wonderfully refreshing, juicy, and crunchy dish would work really well as part of an alfresco feast and can be enjoyed alongside a simple cucumber and radish salad.

Finely shred the cabbage. You can do that by quickly pulsing it in a food processor, or by using a mandolin first and then roughly chopping it with a knife. In a bowl, combine the cabbage, scallions, dill, carrot, and salt and mix for a few minutes so that the cabbage releases its juices—essential to make the fish cakes stick together and also to give you a lovely juicy crunch when you are consuming them.

Chop the cod into small cubes and add it to the bowl, along with the eggs, cornstarch, and lemon zest and juice. Work the ingredients together thoroughly with your hands to obtain a mixture that sticks together.

Heat enough sunflower oil in a frying pan to shallow-fry the fishcakes—the exact amount depends on the size of your pan, but usually around ¼ cup (60 ml) for a small-medium pan will suffice.

Flatten a heaped tablespoon of the mixture into a patty to form each fishcake and fry for about 4 minutes on each side or until golden and crispy.

Place the cakes on paper towels to absorb any excess oil, and sprinkle with the sea salt flakes for an added salty bite.

Salmon & Caviar
Blini Cake

MAKES 1 CAKE; 8–10 SLICES

—

For the pancakes

2⅓ cups (10½ oz/300 g)
    all-purpose flour

2 pinches of salt

4 tablespoons (2 oz/60 g)
    melted unsalted butter

1 egg

1½ cups (350 ml) milk

1¼ cups (300 ml) boiling water

4 tablespoons (2 oz/60 g)
    unsalted butter, for frying

For the filling

1⅔ cups (14 oz/400 g) thick
    Greek yogurt or sour cream

finely grated zest and juice of
    1 lemon

bunch of dill, finely chopped

2 teaspoons drained and finely
    chopped pink peppercorns
    in brine

4 teaspoons drained and finely
    chopped capers in brine

2 teaspoons drained and
    finely chopped sliced green
    jalapeños in brine

small pinch of salt (optional)

7 oz (200 g) smoked salmon

7 oz (200 g) poached skinless
    fresh salmon fillet

1 large cucumber, thinly sliced

4–6 tablespoons salmon
    caviar

9 oz (250 g) cream cheese

A really indulgent and admittedly slightly old-fashioned dish, this reminds me of some prosperous years our family enjoyed in the 1990s, managing to recover from the blows of the collapsed Soviet regime. While this cake was the star of the show at most family gatherings, I remember vividly the very first time I tasted it at my uncle's and aunt's dinner party. My adult self is pleasantly surprised to think that, as a child, I seemed to have enjoyed the rather sophisticated taste of smoked fish and caviar. Though it risks living up to the cliché of wealthy Russians gorging on pancakes with caviar, I chose to include this recipe here simply because it is undeniably delicious. I mean, what's not to like about a cake made entirely of thin lacy crêpes, layered with fresh herbs, cucumbers, cream cheese, salmon, and caviar? Of course, as with any cake, it should be made for a very special occasion and treated with real awe. You can go retro with the garnishing if you would like to relive the Nineties, or opt for a more contemporary minimalist look as I did here.

To make the pancakes, whisk together the flour, salt, melted butter, egg, milk, and measured boiling water in a large bowl until you get a smooth, runny batter.

Heat a frying pan and melt a teaspoon of the butter in it to grease it. Pour half a medium ladleful of the batter onto the pan and swirl it around until you have a thin, even layer. Fry on one side for 40 seconds–1 minute. Flip and fry on the other side for a further 30 seconds, until cooked through, then transfer to a plate.

Continue until all the batter is used up, stacking the pancakes on the plate—it should make about 30.

To prepare the filling (for adding between the layers of buttery pancakes), mix the yogurt or sour cream with the lemon zest and juice, dill, pink peppercorns, capers, and jalapeños. Taste for seasoning and add the salt, if you like.

To assemble your cake, spread the yogurt mixture between pairs of pancakes, and then alternate with layers of smoked and poached salmon, cucumber, and caviar. Keep stacking them up until you have run out of ingredients. You might have a few pancakes leftover, which is never bad news!

To finish your masterpiece, cover the entire cake with the cream cheese before serving it proudly to your guests. Make sure they all take a moment to admire your creation, and only then cut into it to reveal the beautifully colored layers within.

Mushroom &
Buckwheat Risotto

SERVES 4

—

¾ oz (20 g) dried wild
  mushrooms

scant ½ cup (100 ml) boiling
  water

2 tablespoons sunflower oil

1 small onion, finely diced

14 oz (400 g) cremini
  mushrooms, chopped

2 pinches of salt

4 garlic cloves, grated

1 teaspoon finely chopped
  thyme

1 teaspoon finely chopped
  flat-leaf parsley, plus extra
  to serve

⅔ cup (150 ml) dry white wine

splash of soy sauce

2½ cups (14 oz/400 g) roasted
  buckwheat (see page 12)

2½ cups (600 ml) vegetable
  stock

pat of unsalted butter

pinch of freshly ground
  black pepper

6 tablespoons (1¾ oz/50 g)
  toasted pine nuts, to garnish

dill sprigs, to serve

An old Russian saying goes: "Shchi da kasha pishcha nasha"
(good luck trying to pronounce that one!), which simply means
that Shchi soup (see page 82) and porridge are national staples.
With buckwheat and mushrooms being among the most ancient
ingredients of Slavic cuisine, dating far back into the Middle
Ages, porridge with fried onions, mushrooms, and soft herbs is an
indisputable classic. Indeed, nothing can beat the combination of
sweet, earthy, and woody flavors that these ingredients produce
when mixed together. Thinking of ways to elevate this simple dish,
I felt that all these flavors could be highlighted even more if cooked
together as a risotto, with the addition of garlic, white wine, pine
nuts, and a pungent tarragon pesto. Having served this dish at one
of my supper clubs, I received the best feedback from a guest who
compared eating the dish to a walk through a Siberian wood. Well,
bon appétit and enjoy your promenade!

Soak the wild mushrooms in the measured boiling water for
10–15 minutes.

   In the meantime, Heat the oil in a medium saucepan and fry
the onion over medium heat for a few minutes until translucent
but not yet caramelized. Add the cremini mushrooms and salt and
cook over medium heat for 5–8 minutes until the mushrooms have
released their liquid and it has evaporated.

   Drain the wild mushrooms, reserving the liquid, chop them
roughly, and add to the pan, along with the garlic and herbs. Cook
for 5 minutes, before adding the white wine and soy sauce. Increase
the heat and cook for 5–8 minutes to let the alcohol evaporate, and
then add the buckwheat. Reduce the heat to medium and cook,
stirring frequently, until the buckwheat soaks up all the liquid.

   Mix the mushroom soaking liquid with the vegetable stock,
then start adding it to the pan, a scant ½ cup (100 ml) at a time,
stirring constantly. Let each batch of liquid become absorbed
before adding the next. Continue until all the stock is used up. The
buckwheat should be almost cooked by this stage.

   Turn off the heat and add the butter and black pepper, then
cover firmly with a lid and let the risotto rest for 10 minutes.

For the pesto
¾ cup (3½ oz/100 g) pine nuts
large bunch of flat leaf parsley,
 roughly chopped
palmful of tarragon leaves,
 roughly chopped
1 garlic clove, peeled
generous ¾ cup (200 ml)
 olive oil
finely grated zest and juice
 of ½ lemon, or to taste
2 generous pinches of sea
 salt flakes, or to taste

In the meantime, you can prepare the pesto, which could not be simpler: just process all the ingredients together in a food processor or using a handheld immersion blender. Adjust the seasoning and acidity to taste.

Serve the risotto with a generous sprinkle of toasted pine nuts, a dollop of the pesto, and a few parsley and dill leaves.

Eggplant *Matzo Bake*

While the Soviet Union officially embraced multiculturalism, and the food that I grew up with was indeed reflective of this, *matzo* (or *matzah* or *matza*) was not readily available. Perhaps this had something to do with the fact that, in Jewish culture, matzo is very much connected to religious practices, and religion was not accepted in the atheist Soviet state. So this simple flatbread was a bit of an illicit, guilty pleasure that our family enjoyed. My great-grandma would get big boxes of matzo sent to her from Moscow by her cousin, and these were always kept at the back of the cupboard and never openly displayed. She made some delicious dishes with it, my favorite being a baked matzo omelette, so this dish is a homage to our family "secret" ingredient that elaborates on my grandmother's ideas and also embraces my love of eggplants and harissa (adding a Sephardic Jewish touch to the recipe).

Preheat the oven to 400°F (200°C).

Line a medium-sized loaf pan with parchment paper and drizzle with vegetable oil. Cut the eggplant lengthways into thin slices.

In a cup, mix together the tomato and harissa pastes, coriander, dried mint, and some salt and pepper. Add boiling water until a thick pourable consistency is achieved.

Arrange a layer of eggplant slices in the base of the pan, top with a layer of matzo and a layer of cheese, then smother 2 heaped tablespoons of the sauce over the top. Repeat for 5 more layers until most of the eggplant, all of the matzo, and two-thirds of the cheese are used up and the pan is full. Finish with a final layer of eggplant, pour over the remaining sauce, and top with the remaining cheese.

Bake for 35 minutes. Cut in half and serve with the fresh cilantro leaves.

SERVES 2

—

vegetable oil, for drizzling

1 eggplant

¾ cup (7 oz/200 g) tomato paste

2 tablespoons harissa paste

2 teaspoons toasted and freshly ground coriander seeds (*see* page 31)

1 teaspoon dried mint

2 sheets of matzo, broken to fit the loaf pan

5½ oz (150 g) crumbly cheese, such as feta

salt and freshly ground black pepper

cilantro leaves, to serve

Vegan Bigos *with* Smashed New Potatoes

MAKES 10–12

—

For the bigos

4 portobello mushrooms

2 tablespoons soy sauce, or
   more if needed

2 tablespoons good-quality
   unrefined sunflower oil

1 tablespoon mild vegetable oil

1 onion, thinly sliced

1 carrot, peeled and grated

½ white cabbage, shredded

¾ cup (7 oz/200 g) good-
   quality white cabbage
   sauerkraut

generous ¾ cup (200 ml)
   vegetable stock

2 bay leaves

salt and freshly ground
   black pepper

For the smashed potatoes

16–20 new potatoes or other
   small potatoes, scrubbed

scant ½ cup (100 ml)
   good-quality unrefined
   sunflower oil

2 large garlic cloves, crushed

large bunch of dill, finely
   chopped (2 full palmfuls
   when chopped)

salt

While indisputably Polish in its DNA, *bigos* has always been the beloved adopted child in my family. Made by my grandmother and my mom on a regular basis for as long as I can remember, this wonderful stew of sauerkraut, bacon, mushrooms, and dill became an instant hit at one of my pop-up dinners, where I (sacrilegiously) made a vegan version and served it with smashed new potatoes and a richly flavored dill oil. Trust me, it tasted as good as the original, if not better. My secret was the addition of rye croutons steeped in lots of garlic and smoked paprika oil—hello vegan bacon! While this is essentially a peasant dish (code for a delicious but ugly-looking one), when plated in the right way and elevated with a few herbs and seeds, to my eye it always has a subtle autumnal allure.

I encourage you to use homemade sauerkraut here, but if you don't have any around (oh shock, oh horror), try to buy a good-quality brand.

Preheat the oven to 400°F (200°C).

Peel and slice the portobello mushrooms into strips. Place in an oven dish and sprinkle with the soy sauce, a small pinch of salt, and the sunflower oil. Give them a good shake to ensure they are coated evenly and add more soy sauce if the mushrooms look a bit dry. Send them to the oven to roast for 20 minutes.

Meanwhile, heat a lidded heavy-based frying pan or Dutch oven, then add your vegetable oil. Let it warm up a little to ensure the onion and carrot start sizzling as soon as they hit the oil. Add a pinch of salt, cover, and fry over medium-low heat for about 15 minutes until golden, stirring occasionally.

Add the cabbage to the pan, along with a small pinch of salt and let it cook, covered, over medium heat for 10 minutes, before adding the sauerkraut, stock, and bay leaves. Reduce the heat and let it simmer gently for a further 10 minutes.

This dish really does require a lot of multi-tasking, so ideally you should have all the elements cooking in parallel. Boil your potatoes in a saucepan of salted water for 15–20 minutes or until just cooked. Drain and space them out on a baking pan (you don't want the pan to be overcrowded), then roughly squash each with the

Salt & Time

112

For the smoky croutons
2 garlic cloves, grated
2 teaspoons smoked paprika
2¾ tablespoons good-quality
    unrefined sunflower oil
2 generous pinches of salt
6 slices of rye bread

To garnish
small pinch of toasted and
    ground fennel seeds
    (or Russian Dukkah,
    see page 21)
a few small dill sprigs

bottom of a cup or glass. You want the potatoes to still hold their shape and not be completely mashed; this way you will get a nice crispness around the edges and a soft texture in the middle.

In a small bowl, mix together the sunflower oil, garlic, dill, and 2 pinches of salt. Pour over the potatoes, give them a gentle stir to ensure an even coating, and roast for 30 minutes until crisped up.

The mushrooms should be ready by this point. Transfer them from the baking dish to the pot with the cabbage stew. Turn off the heat and let the flavors infuse further.

Finally, make your croutons (if you have the energy to do so or to continue reading this recipe). In a bowl, mix together the garlic, paprika, oil, and salt. Cut the rye bread into lardon-shaped chunks and toss them about in the oil mixture so that they absorb it. Tip out onto a baking pan and toast in the oven for 10 minutes until they crisp up and have absorbed most of the oil. They should be ready at the same time as the potatoes. Make sure to rest them on paper towels so the excess oil can be absorbed.

Dish out an equal amount of potatoes and cabbage stew, top with a handful of mushroom strips, and scatter with the croutons. Add the final touch with a light sprinkle of toasted fennel seeds (or dukkah) and just a little dill for color.

As with any dish containing sauerkraut, this will taste even better after 24 hours, although in my case this incredibly delicious thing never sees the light of the next day.

Plov

SERVES 6–8

—

2½–2¾ cups (1 lb/500 g)
  rice—traditionally devzira,
  but arborio can be used
  instead

scant ½ cup (100 ml) mild
  vegetable oil

1¾ lb (800 g) cubed boneless
  lamb shoulder

2 large onions, thinly sliced
  into half-rings

3–4 carrots, peeled and cut
  into batons

1 large garlic bulb

2 teaspoons cumin seeds,
  toasted and roughly crushed

1 teaspoon coriander seeds,
  roughly crushed

½ teaspoon cayenne pepper

½ teaspoon freshly ground
  black pepper

a few saffron threads

1 tablespoon dried barberries

1 tablespoon salt, or more
  to taste

Plov (or pilau) needs no introduction. Originating in India and Persia, this fragrant meat and rice dish became widespread in Central Asia and the Caucasus and has myriad variations. The type of plov popular in Russia is of the Kazakh and Uzbek varieties. Coming from a city that is only a five-hour drive away from Kazakhstan (a distance that by Russian standards means "just around the corner"), I've been lucky to try some of the most wonderful plovs made with authentic fragrant Asian spices. The preparation of plov is a sacred ceremony, albeit a sexist one, since traditionally only men are allowed to make it. However, the plov I remember the most was made by my aunt, in a giant cast-iron *kazan* (the traditional cookware for this dish) on an open fire. The best part of the dish for me is the indescribably rich and sweet garlic that is cooked whole in the very middle of the kazan. If you can make plov on an open fire, please do, but the recipe below works just fine for an indoor kitchen using a cast-iron pot.

Wash the rice under tepid water until the water runs clear of starch, then soak in warm water while you prepare the rest of the dish.

Heat the oil in a Dutch oven or cast-iron pot and fry the lamb over medium heat until it's golden on all sides, stirring occasionally. This should take 10–15 minutes. Add the onions and carrots and fry for 10 minutes, stirring occasionally. Cover with boiling water so that the meat and vegetables are fully submerged—the exact volume of water depends on the size of your pot.

Place the garlic bulb in the middle of the pot and add the rest of the spices, barberries, and salt. Do not cover, but bring to a boil. Then reduce the heat to a minimum and simmer for 30–40 minutes. This rich golden stock is called *zirak*, in which the rice will be cooked at the next stage.

Drain the rice and add to the pot in a layer on top, without mixing the contents of the pot. Gently submerge the rice in the zirak using a flat slotted spoon. If there isn't enough liquid, top it up with more boiling water so that the rice is covered with at least ½ inch (1 cm) of liquid. You can also add more salt at this stage.

Firmly cover the pot and cook over low heat for 25–30 minutes. If you notice that the plov is only bubbling away in the center, gently push the rice from the edges towards the middle. Turn out onto a platter and serve with seasonal vegetables and soft herbs.

Millet Risotto *with* Pancetta & Sage Butter

SERVES 4

—

7 oz (200 g) pancetta, diced
(leave out for a vegetarian
version)

1 onion, finely diced

2 celery sticks, finely diced

1 carrot, peeled and finely
diced

small bunch of flat leaf parsley,
chopped

1½ cups (10½ oz/300 g) millet

3 cups (700 ml) vegetable
stock or water, plus extra if
needed

1½ tablespoons (¾ oz/20 g)
unsalted butter (optional)

2 tablespoons olive oil

¾ cup (3½ oz/100 g) blanched
hazelnuts, roasted and finely
chopped

7 oz (200 g) feta cheese,
crumbled (optional, but
recommended for the
vegetarian version)

salt and freshly ground
black pepper

For the sage butter

7 tablespoons (3½ oz/100 g)
unsalted butter

handful of sage leaves, plus
extra to serve

sea salt flakes

Millet porridge was a widespread gastronomic torture device in most Soviet kindergartens and school cafeterias. But when cooked in the right way, it is one of the most delicious and nutrient-rich grains traditional to Russian cuisine, which can easily rival couscous for flavor and versatility of use. Characterized by its bright yellow color, sweet taste, and creamy texture, it can be used in both sweet and savory dishes. In this recipe, I use some of the traditional ingredients and vamp them up a bit to create a dish that is rich in flavor and texture, as well as being pleasant on the eye.

Heat a medium saucepan or Dutch oven over medium heat and fry the pancetta, if using, without any oil, for 10 minutes or until it starts to crisp up and releases most of its fat.

Next, add the onion, celery, and carrot and fry for 5–8 minutes until the vegetables soften. You can add some salt at this point if you are going to use water rather than a vegetable stock that is already seasoned.

Add the parsley and fry for about a minute before adding the millet. Stir through to make sure the vegetables and the pancetta are evenly mixed, and then top with the vegetable stock or water.

Cook, uncovered, over medium heat for 20–25 minutes, stirring occasionally. If you see that the stock has been absorbed but the millet is still undercooked, add an extra ¾ cup (180 ml) or so of stock or water.

Once the porridge is cooked, turn off the heat, add the butter if you want to give it some extra creaminess, and season with salt and pepper to taste. Stir, then tightly cover the pot and let the porridge sit for 20 minutes.

Make the sage butter by melting the butter in a pan over low heat. Once it starts to bubble, add the sage leaves and fry for 1–2 minutes or until they crisp up, then sprinkle with sea salt flakes.

To serve, divide the porridge among 4 plates. Sprinkle with the roasted hazelnuts and a few sage leaves, then drizzle the sage butter all over. If you have gone the veggie route and omitted the pancetta, I would highly recommend crumbling some feta on top to add a bit of extra saltiness and creaminess.

Golubtsy for the Lazy: a Layered Cabbage Pie

MAKES 1 PIE; SERVES 6–8

—

1 white cabbage

mild vegetable oil, for frying
    and oiling

1 onion, diced

1 carrot, peeled and grated

4 garlic cloves, grated

bunch of dill, finely chopped

9 oz (250 g) ground beef

2 tablespoons tomato paste

⅓ cup (80 ml) hot water

½ tablespoon brown sugar

1 teaspoon smoked paprika

½ teaspoon ground nutmeg

1 teaspoon red pepper flakes

2 cups (7 oz/200 g) white
    mushrooms, roughly
    chopped

small bunch of flat leaf parsley,
    chopped

⅔ cup (4¼ oz/120g) basmati
    rice

salt and freshly ground
    black pepper

sour cream, to serve

For the crumbs (optional)

1 tablespoon sunflower oil

7 oz (200 g) pancetta or bacon
    lardons

1 garlic clove, grated

2 large slices of dense rye
    bread, cut into cubes

I've come to realize that cabbage has a bad reputation here. The quintessential symbol of bad and smelly Eastern European cuisine, this nutrient-rich brassica is generally named as the main reason why some people dislike or are not keen to try Russian food. Well, I am here to dispel this stereotype. I absolutely love cabbage in all its guises (yes, even the scent of boiled cabbage makes me go "yum!"), from *borsch* and *shchi* soups (*see* pages 70 and 82), to sauerkraut (*see* pages 159 and 160) and, of course, stuffed cabbage leaves. Known across Eastern Europe and Russia as "little pigeons," *golubtsy* are widely consumed in most households. But despite their popularity, they are quite a time-consuming dish to create. So I've decided to make this crustless cabbage pie instead, a sort of a "golubtsy for the lazy." As I've since discovered, there are similar dishes in Balkan and Hungarian cuisines—what can I say, there is a lazy cook in all of us. What I particularly like about this version is that you can combine different flavors and add as many layers as you like, adhering to the old Russian tradition of multi-tiered savory pies. Serve it with this bacon and rye crumb, and then try telling me you don't like cabbage!

In this cake, the cabbage leaves play the part of pastry, so we will need to peel them off first. In order to do that, cut off the stem base and braise the cabbage, intact, in a pot of salted boiling water for 10–15 minutes.

While the cabbage is cooking, prepare the fillings. To make the meat mixture, heat up a tablespoon of oil in a pot and fry the onion, carrot, half of the garlic, and the dill over medium heat for 8–10 minutes. Add the ground beef and fry for 5–8 minutes until the meat is cooked throughout and begins to turn golden, adding a splash of water if it starts to catch too much. Then stir in the tomato paste and measured hot water to create a rich sauce, and season it with salt and pepper to taste (2 pinches of each should be enough), followed by the sugar and all of the spices. Cover with a lid and simmer over low heat for 10–15 minutes.

In the meantime, make the mushroom and rice mixture. Heat up a frying pan and cook the mushrooms with a tablespoon of oil, a good pinch of salt, the remaining garlic, and the parsley over medium heat for 5 minutes, covered, until the mushrooms have released their juices. Remove from the heat. Stir in the rice, along with a few tablespoons of hot water if the mixture feels too dry.

By this point your cabbage should be ready. Drain and let it cool for a few minutes before starting to peel off the leaves. A medium-sized cabbage usually yields around 20 medium-sized leaves.

Meanwhile, preheat the oven to 400°F (200°C).

Oil a round springform cake pan and cover the base and sides with a layer of cabbage leaves as neatly as you can. The leaves should be supple and mold into the pan quite easily. Start building your tiers by adding a layer of the meat mixture (the amount will depend on the size of your pan), followed by a layer of cabbage leaves. The next tier will be made up of the mushroom and rice mixture, followed by a final layer of the cabbage leaves to seal the cake. If the pan you are using is smaller in circumference but quite deep, you can keep going until you have run out of the fillings and cabbage leaves.

Brush the pie with oil and bake, uncovered, for 20–30 minutes, until the leaves become crisp in places. Let the pie cool down slightly before opening the springform ring and carefully sliding the pie onto a plate or a wooden board.

To make the crumbs, heat the oil in a frying pan and fry the pancetta or bacon over medium heat until all the fat has melted and the meat begins to caramelize. This should take 10–15 minutes. Add the garlic and rye bread cubes and fry for a further 5 minutes until the bread soaks up the fat and starts to crisp up. The mixture should be crisp enough to be whizzed into crumbs without turning into a paste. You can either use a good food processor to crumb the mixture, in which case you will need to pulse it for about 30 seconds, or simply chop it up with a knife until it reaches a fine, crumbly consistency.

Serve the pie with a side of bacon and rye crumbs and a bowl of sour cream (feel free to spinkle extra crumbs on top of the sour cream too).

Squid Poached *in* Smetana Sauce

—

1 tablespoon sunflower oil

2 onions, thinly sliced into
   half-rings

4 carrots, peeled and grated

2 tablespoons soy sauce

1¾ cups (14 oz/400 g)
   smetana (*see* page 13) or
   sour cream

1 bay leaf

1 lb (500 g) cleaned squid
   tubes (bodies), thinly sliced
   into rings

salt and freshly ground
   black pepper

handful of flat-leaf parsley
   leaves, to garnish (optional)

This is the ultimate comfort dish from my childhood. My mom has been making it regularly for as long as I can remember, and both my dad and I never turned down the opportunity to devour it for lunch or dinner. The soy sauce adds a certain touch of something "exotic" to the other more traditional Russian-tasting ingredients, which create a pleasant complexity of sweet and tangy flavors. The dish looks really scrumptious and comforting, and I often think of it as a Russian curry, thanks to its beautifully golden and rich sauce.

This dish could not be easier to make and is so satisfying in its simplicity. It goes well with jasmine rice or some good old mashed potatoes (to which I am highly partial).

Heat the oil in a cast-iron sauté pan or a large frying pan with a lid. Add the onions, carrots, and a pinch of salt and fry over medium heat for 5–7 minutes until the vegetables soften and turn golden.

Add the soy sauce, sour cream, and bay leaf. Reduce the heat and gently bring to a vigorous simmer. Make sure that the sauce doesn't start boiling vigorously, or the sour cream will curdle. Once the sauce is on the verge of boiling, add the squid rings and poach for 7 minutes. Taste the sauce and season accordingly with salt and black pepper. Sprinkle with some parsley leaves, if you like, and a bit more black pepper before serving.

Kurnik Chicken Pie

MAKES 1 PIE; SERVES 8–10

—

For the pastry

3 cups (13 oz/375 g) all-
purpose flour, plus extra
for dusting

½ teaspoon salt

2 sticks and 5 tablespoons
(10½ oz/300 g) chilled
unsalted butter, cubed

⅓ cup (3 oz/85 g) sour cream

1 egg, beaten, to seal and glaze

For the filling

3½ tablespoons (1¾ oz/50 g)
unsalted butter

3 onions, thinly sliced

4 carrots, peeled and grated

14 oz (400 g) boneless chicken
thighs, skinless or skin on,
as you prefer

1⅓ cups (9 oz/250 g) long-
grain white rice

6 hard-boiled eggs, peeled

small bunch chives, finely
chopped

small bunch tarragon, finely
chopped

small bunch dill, finely chopped

generous ¾ cup (200 ml) hot
chicken broth (*see* page 90)

salt and freshly ground
black pepper

Russians love their pies and have invented a whole range of them:
starting with small *pirozhki* (*see* page 42) and open-faced pies of all
sizes like *rastegai, shanga,* and *vatrushka;* followed by single-tier
closed *pirog* (not to be confused with Polish dumplings). The list
culminates in show-stopping multi-layered *koulebiaka* and *kurnik*
pies. While koulebiaka is usually made with fish (*see* page 130),
kurnik (from the Russian word *kuritsa,* meaning "chicken") is made
with poultry and served with a side of hot chicken broth. With its
distinctive domed shape, resembling an ancient Russian wooden hut,
this pie would be an exotic treat on any contemporary table.

To make the most tender flaky pastry, you will need to pulse the
flour, salt, and butter together in a food processor until you have
uniform crumbs with no lumps of butter within the flour. Add the
sour cream and pulse again until the dough starts to form a ball.
Tip onto a work surface and gently bring together with your hands.
Cut off roughly one-third of the pastry dough and shape into a disc.
Shape the remaining two-thirds of dough into another disc. Wrap
both discs individually in plastic wrap and chill in the refrigerator for
about an hour until firm.

Next, cook all the ingredients for the filling. Melt 2 tablespoons
(1 oz/30 g) of the butter in a large frying pan over low heat and
fry the onions and carrots, with a generous sprinkling of salt, for
10–15 minutes until they begin to caramelize, stirring occasionally.
Remove from the pan and set aside.

In the same pan, melt the remaining butter and fry the chicken
thighs over medium heat for 6–8 minutes on each side, seasoning
with salt and pepper as you turn. If using thighs with skin, make sure
to get it nice and crispy. Let them cool slightly before pulling the
chicken apart with your fingers—you want juicy bite-sized chunks
or strips.

Cook the rice in plenty of salted boiling water for a minute or so
less than the package instructions—you want it to be al dente, since
it will cook further once inside the pie. Drain and let it cool.

Roughly chop the hard-boiled eggs and mix them with all the
herbs. Season generously with salt and pepper.

Now your pastry is ready for action!

Line a large (12 cup/3 liter) bowl with plastic wrap, making sure there is a bit of overhang around the sides. Remove the bigger disc of pastry from the refrigerator and lightly flour your work surface. Roll out the disc into a rough circle until it's about ⅛ inch (3 mm) thick and use it to carefully line your plastic-covered bowl, ensuring there are no air pockets between the bowl and the pastry. Return to the refrigerator while you roll out the smaller disc in a circle to the same thickness.

When the filling ingredients are sufficiently cool, remove the pastry-lined bowl from the refrigerator and start layering, beginning with the herby eggs, followed by the onions and carrots, the chicken, and finally the rice. Make sure you firmly pack down each layer before adding the next, since this helps the pie to hold its shape once you flip it and remove the bowl.

Brush the pastry rim with some of the beaten egg (reserve the rest for later) and top the pie with the smaller pastry disc. Pinch together to seal, leaving the overhang. Chill the pie in the refrigerator for a couple of hours.

When you're ready to bake the pie, preheat the oven to 400°F (200°C) and line a baking pan with parchment paper. Place the pan on top of the bowl, paper-side down. Holding the base of the bowl, quickly flip it and the baking pan over together, then carefully remove the bowl and plastic wrap to reveal your pie.

Trim and crimp or twist the edges, then brush the whole pie with the remaining beaten egg. If you have any dough left over, you can also add some ornate shapes to decorate the pie and give it a folksy Russian look. Use a knife to cut a cross in the top to allow the steam to escape. Bake for 1 hour 20 minutes or until golden brown and a metal skewer inserted into the steam hole comes out hot.

Bring the whole pie to the table and add an element of performance by pouring the hot chicken broth into the hole at the top. Alternatively, enjoy a slice of the pie with a steaming mug of broth on the side.

Koulebiaka Salmon Pie

MAKES 1 PIE; SERVES 14–16

—

1 quantity of pastry dough
  (*see* page 126)

all-purpose flour, for dusting

For the filling

1 stick (4 oz/115 g) unsalted
  butter

4 onions, sliced into half-rings

3 cups (1 lb/500 g) roasted
  buckwheat (*see* page 12)

5 cups (1 lb/500 g) cremini
  mushrooms, roughly
  chopped

2 garlic cloves, grated

small bunch of flat-leaf
  parsley, finely chopped

generous ¾ cup (200 ml)
  heavy cream

1 lb (500 g) skinless salmon
  fillet

bunch of dill, chopped

6 hard-boiled eggs, peeled
  and roughly chopped

bunch of chives, finely
  chopped

1 egg, beaten, to glaze

salt and freshly ground
  black pepper

This is another example of how Russians tend to push the boat out when it comes to pies! An old dish of pre-Revolutionary cuisine that is still enjoyed today, *koulebiaka* is made with a light pastry that encases layer upon layer of fish, grains, eggs, mushrooms, herbs, and creamy sauce. This pie is both mesmerizing and nutrient-rich—you won't need anything else at the table apart from your hungry dinner companions!

This is a real labor of love kind of dish, so make sure you have plenty of time to indulge in the tricky yet amazingly satisfying ritual. Just think of the gorgeous show-stopping centerpiece that will adorn your table and of all the gasps of your fellow diners!

Start by making the pastry dough, following the recipe on page 126. While the dough is resting, make the filling.

Melt half of the butter in a frying pan over low heat and cook the onions with a bit of salt for 10–15 minutes, stirring occasionally. You want them to be soft, sweet, and slightly caramelized.

Cook the buckwheat following the recipe on page 34, then mix it with the onions, making sure not to lose any of that golden butter.

Next, prepare the mushroom filling. Melt the remaining butter in a frying pan and fry the mushrooms, garlic, parsley, and a pinch of salt over medium heat for 8–10 minutes. Turn off the heat and stir in the cream. Add a good pinch of pepper, cover with a lid, and let the mixture infuse while you prepare the rest of the dish.

Cut the salmon fillet into bite-sized chunks, then mix with the dill, and salt and pepper to taste. Set aside. Roughly chop the hard-boiled eggs and mix them with the chives, and salt and pepper to taste.

Now, you are ready to assemble the beauty! Spread a large sheet of parchment paper onto a baking pan and dust it with some flour. Roll out 10½–12 oz (300–350 g) of the pastry dough (a little less than half) on the floured sheet into a rectangle about ¼ inch (5 mm) thick and then start layering the koulebiaka. Add the buckwheat and onion mixture first and shape it into a rectangle, leaving a border of pastry about ¾ inch (2 cm) wide around all the edges. Next, add a layer of the salmon and dill, followed by the creamy mushrooms. If you find there is too much of the sauce, reserve it and serve it alongside the finished pie. Finish with a layer of the egg and chive mixture.

Roll out the remaining pastry dough into a rectangle slightly larger than the first and cover the pie with it. Seal the edges tightly by twisting and pinching the 2 sheets of dough together.

Let the pie rest at room temperature for 30 minutes, while you preheat the oven to 350°F (180°C). Brush the pastry generously with beaten egg and bake for 45 minutes–1 hour until golden brown. Serve the whole thing on a big platter and slice at the table for that extra "wow factor."

A Trout & Potato Stew
in *Gorshochki Pots*

SERVES 4

—

1 tablespoon sunflower oil

4 potatoes, peeled and cut into small cubes

1 carrot, peeled and cut into medium-thick discs

small bunch of scallions, thinly sliced

½ small bunch flat-leaf parsley, finely chopped

½ small bunch dill, finely chopped

4 bay leaves

½ onion, thinly sliced into half-rings

2 large rainbow trout fillets, skinned and cut into bite-sized chunks

4–6 lemon slices

generous ¾ cup (200 ml) vegetable or fish stock

sea salt flakes and freshly ground black pepper

Every national cuisine has its own equivalent of Russian *gorshochki*: clay, cast-iron, or ceramic pots used for cooking a wide range of foods. While this method was initially employed to cook on an open fire, gorshochki pots are firmly associated with the traditional wood-fired oven—the true heart and soul of the rural Russian household and an iconic feature in numerous fables and fairy tales. Varying in size from large enough to feed an entire family, to individual ones, the particular shape of gorshochki, akin to a honey pot, creates a special microclimate that results in wonderfully moist and tender dishes. While here I offer you a recipe featuring trout, you can cook any other fish as well as meat or poultry using a similar method. Adding some sour cream to the pot will create an even more nourishing and comforting dish.

While the essence of this dish is the very clay pot in which it is cooked, you can achieve a rather tasty result if you cook it in a different vessel—one medium-sized Dutch oven or lidded casserole dish, or 4 small individual cocottes. As long as there is a lid to seal the deal, you and your trout should be perfectly fine.

Preheat the oven to 350°F (180°C).

Drizzle the base of your cooking vessel or vessels with the sunflower oil and layer the vegetables and fish in 2 identical tiers: starting with the potatoes and carrot, then the scallions, chopped herbs (reserving ½ tablespoon of each for adding later), and the bay leaves, then finishing with the onion and trout. Finish assembling the dish with a layer of lemon slices, a sprinkle of sea salt and black pepper, and the remaining tablespoon of chopped herbs.

Pour the stock into the pot (or pots), cover with the lid (or lids), and bake for 40 minutes–1 hour. The best part of this dish is the moment when you open the lid and let the incredible aroma make your head spin!

Fern Stir-fry

A few years ago, a foodie friend of mine asked me to recall my favorite family dish. Without any hesitation I said "My mom's fern stir-fry." This caused a wave of surprised laughter and the comment: "You guys in Siberia are weird!" Puzzled by such a reaction, I started to look into the origin of the dish that was so dear to my heart. As it turned out, this was indeed a rather unusual one, even by Russian standards. In Russia, edible fiddlehead fern is common only in the Russian Far East, a culinary influence from China and Korea, and it was my dad's mom who used to send us parcels of brined fern from the Far East back in the late 1980s and 1990s. While fern gradually became more popular all over the country, it is still relatively rare today and can only be found at specialist Korean market stalls, where it is sold alongside other pickled and brined delights. While you can try to imitate fern's unique flavor and texture by stir-frying some white mushrooms and asparagus spears instead, I can't encourage you enough to try and obtain the original from East Asian grocery stores or, when in season, buy it fresh from farmers' markets or ask an experienced forager to pick some for you.

Heat the oil in a large frying pan.

Pat the beef dry and season with a pinch of salt. Fry the meat in the hot oil over medium-high heat for 10 minutes until it is seared on both sides.

Add the onion, red pepper, and soy sauce and fry, stirring occasionally, for 5–8 minutes.

Add the fiddleheads, garlic, and red pepper flakes, mix well, and cook for a further 15 minutes. If you are using mushrooms and asparagus instead, then reduce the cooking time at this stage to 7–10 minutes.

Season with salt to taste and serve hot. This dish works perfectly well on its own, or you can add a side of mashed potatoes, as we always did in our family.

SERVES 4

—

1 tablespoon mild vegetable oil

1 lb (500 g) boneless stewing steak, cut into strips

1 onion, thinly sliced

1 red pepper, cored, deseeded and thinly sliced

¼ cup (60 ml) soy sauce

14 oz (400 g) brined Asian ferns or fresh edible fiddlehead ferns

4 garlic cloves, grated

1 teaspoon red pepper flakes

salt

Salt & Time

136

"Hedgehog" Meatballs *in* Creamy Mushroom Sauce

Without a doubt, this used to be my best-loved meal when I was little, so I would highly recommended it to any parent of a fussy, young eater. I think it was the name of the dish that made it especially appealing to me. A huge fan of the most wonderful Soviet cartoon *A Hedgehog in the Fog*, I found an odd delight in thinking that these rice-studded meatballs, floating in a creamy sauce, were just like my favorite cartoon character who gets lost in the fog. To this day, the dish remains a favorite for a lazy dinner at my parents' house, and I have never seen my dad turn it down. Perhaps there is also a child in him who draws a slightly odd parallel between this dish and an iconic Soviet cartoon character. Serve them with mashed potatoes.

To make the "hedgehogs," mix the ground beef with the onion, garlic, rice, and parsley in a large bowl, and season with salt and pepper. Use 2 heaped tablespoons to form each "hedgehog" or meatball. You should end up with 12. Set aside or refrigerate while you make the sauce.

   Heat the oil in a large sauté pan and fry the mushrooms and onion over medium heat for 5–8 minutes. Add the cream and stock, season with salt and pepper to taste, and cook for a further 8 minutes over very low heat.

   While the sauce is simmering, cook the meatballs. Heat the oil in a heavy-based frying pan or cast-iron sauté pan and cook the meatballs for 40 seconds–1 minute on each side until they get a lovely crispy coating. Add the mushroom sauce, reduce the heat, and simmer for 10 minutes.

   These "hedgehogs" simply must be served with the fluffiest mashed potatoes and plenty of the creamy sauce to pour all over your plate.

SERVES 4–6

—

For the meatballs
1 lb (500 g) ground beef
1 onion, finely diced
2 garlic cloves, grated
generous ½ cup (3½ oz/100 g) basmati rice
1 tablespoon mild vegetable oil, for frying
salt and freshly ground black pepper

For the sauce
1 tablespoon sunflower oil
2 cups (7 oz/200 g) white mushrooms, finely sliced
½ onion, finely diced
1 cup (250 ml) light cream
generous ¾ cup (200 ml) stock (a ready-made vegetable stock would work here)
2 tablespoons finely chopped flat-leaf parsley
salt and freshly ground black pepper

Siberian *Pelmeni Dumplings*

MAKES ABOUT 200 DUMPLINGS;
SERVES 10

—

For the dough

3 cups (1 lb 8 oz/700 g) Italian
"00" flour, plus extra
for dusting

1 teaspoon salt

2 eggs

generous ¾ cup (200 ml)
water

For the meat filling option

9 oz (250 g) ground pork

9 oz (250 g) ground beef

1 onion, very finely chopped

1 teaspoon salt

1 teaspoon freshly ground
black pepper

For the fish filling option

12 oz (340 g) skinless salmon
fillet, cut into small pieces

12 oz (340 g) skinless trout
fillet, cut into small pieces

12 oz (340 g) skinless cod
fillet, cut into small pieces

1 onion, very finely chopped

2 garlic cloves, grated

bunch of chives, finely
chopped

1 teaspoon salt

1 teaspoon freshly ground
black pepper

There is something universal about dumplings—we all connect over our shared love of boiled dough stuffed with a filling of sorts. While there are so many types of dumplings native to different parts of the former Soviet Union, Siberia's claim to fame is its own signature type called Siberian *pelmeni*. These tiny round dumplings are often stuffed with a blend of ground pork and beef and are consumed with a generous chunk of butter, black pepper, and sour cream or—and this is my family's favorite—in their own richly flavored cooking broth, with plenty of black pepper, of course! My dad would often have these (as well as pretty much anything else) with soy sauce that his mother would send us from his home town of Khabarovsk way before it became widely available in shops all over Russia. Since pelmeni were usually eaten in winter when no fresh herbs were available, adding fresh dill was not common practice, but I would highly recommend this to you these days, as well as experimenting with other non-Russian herbs. Pelmeni in sage butter, anyone? I have provided three filling options here; choose one to fill this quantity of dough.

To make the dough, sift the flour onto a clean, dry work surface. Make a well in the middle and add the salt, eggs, and measured water, gradually mixing the flour into it with your hands to form a firm dough. Knead well for 5–7 minutes. Cover with plastic wrap and let it rest in the refrigerator for 30 minutes. In the meantime, prepare your chosen filling.

If you chose the meat or fish filling, thoroughly mix the respective ingredients together in a large bowl.

To make the mushroom filling, finely chop the mushrooms, onion, garlic, and parsley in a food processor. Heat the oil in a large frying pan and fry the vegetable mixture with the soy sauce for 5 minutes. Turn off the heat and stir in the pine nuts, salt, and pepper. Let the mixture cool before handling.

The dough should be ready by this point. Take it out of the refrigerator and roll it out on a lightly floured work surface. For best results, use a pasta machine, since you need to make sheets that are about 1.5 mm thick, which you will get by using a number 7 setting on your pasta machine.

For the mushroom filling option

14 oz (400 g) mixed
   mushrooms (wild
   mushrooms, or a mixture
   of white and cremini
   mushrooms)
1 onion, quartered
2 garlic cloves
small bunch of flat-leaf
   parsley, finely chopped
2 tablespoons sunflower oil
dash of soy sauce
generous 1 cup (5½ oz/150 g)
   pine nuts
1 teaspoon salt
1 teaspoon freshly ground
black pepper

For the cooking broth

1 bay leaf
1 vegetable, fish, or meat
   bouillon cube, according to
   your filling

To serve

unsalted butter (if serving
   without the cooking broth)
chopped fresh herbs
sour cream
freshly ground black pepper

Using a shot glass or cookie cutter, cut out discs of dough, 1½–2½ inches (4–6 cm) in diameter. Place a teaspoon of your filling in the middle of each disc and fold in half to make a half-moon shape, then fold again so that the edges of the half-moon are stuck together.

The dumplings can be cooked immediately or frozen to be cooked at a later date using the same method as below, increasing the cooking time as necessary.

To cook, bring a large saucepan of salted water to a boil, adding the bay leaf and bouillon cube. Add the pelmeni, in batches, to the boiling broth and cook for 5 minutes per batch. You know they are ready when they float up to the surface.

Ladle your pelmeni into soup bowls with the cooking broth, topping them with fresh herbs, sour cream, and black pepper. If you prefer to have them without the broth, transfer them to the bowls using a slotted spoon and add a generous dollop of butter, as well as the rest of the serving ingredients. This makes around 10 servings of dumplings, but if that's more than the number of mouths that you have to feed, they freeze well kept in flat layers in a freezer bag.

Chicken *with* Prunes

SERVES 4

—

2 tablespoons oil, for frying

4 chicken legs

3½ tablespoons (1¾ oz/50 g)
    unsalted butter

6 banana shallots, halved
    lengthways

½ cup (120 ml) red wine

½ cup (120 ml) chicken stock

1 tablespoon herbes de
    Provence

¾ cup (4½ oz/125 g) pitted
    prunes, roughly chopped

At one of my recent catering jobs, I was asked to create a menu themed around the Soviet Space Race. Never being a person to shy away from in-depth research, I delved into a vast body of sources dedicated to the nutrition of Soviet cosmonauts. One scientific article in particular caught my eye. On the one hand, it was amazingly boring, but on the other it was perfect—a detailed comparative study of the calorific intake of the Soviet and American spacemen and women. As soon as I saw a dish on the Soviet menu called chicken with prunes, my imagination ran wild. I knew immediately that in my version I had to have lots of butter, shallots, red wine, and fragrant herbs to create a decadently rich, tangy, and sweet dish, which most definitely tastes nothing like what the Soviets ate up there in space. But hey, I am sure my guests here on planet Earth were very happy about that.

This dish is best served with creamy mashed potatoes, and make sure to have a big chunk of sourdough bread to mop up the seductively rich sauce.

Preheat the oven to 425°F (220°C).

Heat the oil in a large ovenproof frying pan over medium heat and fry the chicken legs, skin side down, for 5 minutes to achieve a nice golden color. Transfer the chicken to a plate and set aside while you make the sauce.

Melt the butter in the same pan and, as it starts to bubble, add the shallots cut sides down. Fry for 5 minutes or until almost all the butter has been absorbed. Deglaze the pan with the red wine and let the alcohol evaporate by increasing the heat for a minute. At this point, your kitchen will be filled with the most intoxicating aroma! Make sure to have a glass of red wine on the side for yourself.

Next, add the chicken stock, herbs, and prunes and reduce the stock over high heat for 2–3 minutes.

Return the chicken legs to the pan, crispy skin up, transfer to the oven, and cook for 20 minutes or until the juices run clear when pierced with a toothpick.

Steak *with* Black Radish Rémoulade

Initially, this dish was meant to go into the salad chapter, since it is indeed based on a very popular winter salad of black radish, fried onions, and beef in mayo. In my family it is only served around the New Year's festivities and is always a hit. But although this is traditionally a Soviet appetizer, usually eaten with bread, I simply couldn't bring myself to place such a deeply nutritious number in an opening chapter. Moreover, I believe a good slice of meat deserves to be displayed and admired solo, with the mayo-dressed vegetables acting to enhance the look and flavor of the meat and not to mask it. Make sure to cast the best-quality meat in the leading role and you are guaranteed to have a truly spectacular main course.

Heat the oil in a large frying pan over medium heat, then add the onions, ensuring the oil is hot enough that they sizzle straight away. Add the small pinch of salt, reduce the heat, and cook for 15 minutes until the onions are soft, golden, and sweet, stirring occasionally.

While the onions are getting to the desired state, peel and julienne the celeriac and radish. Set aside.

Make the dressing by combining the crème fraîche with the mustard, vinegar, lemon juice, sea salt, and black pepper.

Once the onions have cooked, let them cool down, then mix them with the radish and celeriac and stir in the dressing. Taste and adjust the seasoning and acidity to your palate—the rémoulade should be quite creamy but also have a bit of a sharp edge to it.

In order to cook a perfect steak, you need to season it generously and let it spend the night in the refrigerator. However, it is absolutely essential that you bring it back to room temperature before frying. Get your pan smoking hot and fry each steak for 5 minutes on each side for medium-rare, adding a pat of butter and a bit of salt and pepper at the very end. Let them rest for 5 minutes before serving.

To plate: cut each steak into strips against the grain and place on a plate next to 2 heaped tablespoons of the onion, radish, and celeriac rémoulade, and drop over a few parsley leaves to liven up this elegant dish.

SERVES 4

—

For the rémoulade

2 tablespoons sunflower oil

2 white onions, sliced into
    half-rings

small pinch of salt

1 small celeriac (celery root)

1 small black radish or daikon,
    or ½ if using a large one

4 tablespoons crème fraîche

2 tablespoons Dijon mustard

1 tablespoon white wine
    vinegar

1 tablespoon lemon juice,
    or to taste

good pinch of sea salt flakes

2 teaspoons toasted and
    coarsely ground black
    peppercorns

For the steak

4 good-quality sirloin bavette
    steaks (the weight depends
    on your appetite)

3½ tablespoons (1¾ oz/50 g)
    unsalted butter

sea salt flakes and freshly
    ground black pepper

handful of flat-leaf parsley
    leaves, to garnish

Roast Festive Bird *Two Ways*

Perhaps my culinary fate was sealed when the first word that I had ever uttered at the tender age of six months was "goose." Our family was gathered at the festive table, and as my mom introduced the dish to her guests, I suddenly had no difficulty repeating it after her. A classic winter dish, goose with sauerkraut is served either on New Year's Eve (by which point the guests can hardly breathe, having already devoured an array of salads and appetizers) or on Russian Christmas Eve, ever since the religious holiday became legitimate again in the 1990s following the collapse of the USSR. While goose is a more traditional bird for this treatment, duck also works beautifully, so I would highly recommend giving it a try. Whichever bird you decide to use, make sure to serve it with a side of roast potatoes (cooked in the bird's fat, of course) and you've got yourself a very special winter meal.

Goose *with* Apple, Fennel & Dill Sauerkraut

SERVES 6–8

—

1 medium goose (about
   7¾ lb/3.5 kg)
1 tablespoon sunflower oil
2 large onions, thinly sliced
4¼ cups (2¼ lb/1 kg) Apple,
   Fennel & Dill Sauerkraut
   (*see* page 160)
salt and freshly ground
   black pepper

Remove the goose from the refrigerator and let it rest at room temperature for an hour before cooking.

In the meantime, heat the oil in a large sauté pan or Dutch oven and fry the onions over medium heat for 5 minutes. Add the sauerkraut with its brine, season with some salt and pepper, and braise for 10–15 minutes. Take off the heat and let it cool down slightly.

Preheat the oven to 400°F (200°C).

Pat the goose's cavity dry with paper towels and stuff it with the braised sauerkraut. Pierce the skin on the thighs and breast with a fork and generously season with salt and pepper. Roast in a deep roasting pan for 2½–3 hours. The goose will release a lot of fat, which you can use to baste it as it cooks. To check if the bird is ready to grace the festive table, pierce the thigh and, if the juices run clear, it's good to go!

Make sure to save all that glorious goose fat, which will be perfect for roasting potatoes.

Duck *with* Red Sauerkraut

Remove the duck from the refrigerator and let it rest at room temperature for an hour before cooking.

In the meantime, heat the oil in a large sauté pan or Dutch oven and fry the onions over medium heat for 5 minutes. Add the sauerkraut with its brine, along with the prunes, and cook for 5 minutes. Pour in the wine and braise for 10 minutes. Season with salt and pepper to taste.

Follow the recipe for the goose on the previous page to prepare and roast the duck, but the cooking time will be only 1 hour.

SERVES 4

—

1 medium duck (about
    1¾ lb/800 g)
1 tablespoon sunflower oil
2 large red onions, thinly sliced
2½ cups (1 lb 5 oz/600 g) Red
    Sauerkraut with Garlic &
    Chili (*see* page 159)
1¼ cups (7 oz/200 g) pitted
    prunes, roughly chopped
½ cup (120 ml) red wine
salt and freshly ground
    black pepper

A fall party:

Plov (*see* page 114)

Vegetable Patties with

Dipping Sauces (*see* pages

28–31)

Lavash Wraps (*see* page 40)

Babushka Ganoush

(*see* page 38)

Pickles &
Ferments

Chapter 4

While fermentation has become very popular over recent years in our health-crazed Western world, the tradition of consuming fermented foods (fruit, vegetables, breads, and drinks) dates back to before the Middle Ages in Russia and its appeal remains intact today. Before the discovery of many of the health benefits, generation upon generation of Russians fermented foods as a means of coping with shortages during the colder months, particularly in the days when imported foods were not available. What I love most about food fermentation is the ritual of the process, which endows you with a magical ability to suspend time in a jar using nothing but salt. Cucumbers harvested in the summer or mushrooms picked in early fall will reappear on your table in winter, establishing a beautiful connection between the seasons. The mystery of cooking with nothing but salt and time, for me, lies at the very heart of Russian cuisine. In this chapter, as well as exploring traditional Slavic ferments, I indulge my childhood obsession with Soviet-Korean pickled vegetables.

Fermented Cucumbers

MAKES A HALF-GALLON
(2-LITER) JAR

—

small bunch of celery leaves

8–10 pickling cucumbers such
as Kirby, ends trimmed

4 garlic cloves, peeled

1 small fresh horseradish,
peeled and chopped into
rough chunks

1 Habanero chili pepper,
sliced in half

small bunch of dill

small bunch fresh flat-leaf
parsley

2 teaspoons fennel seeds

2 teaspoons coriander seeds

2 teaspoons black
peppercorns

1 tablespoon fine salt

4¼ cups (1 liter) distilled
spring water

Fermented cucumbers are one of the most iconic foods in Slavic and Soviet cuisine. Prepared in a fragrant salt brine, these are not to be confused with Ashkenazi sugar-and-vinegar pickles. The abundance of aromatics and spices in the brine makes the crunchy cucumber a punchy chaser for a shot of vodka, but also a perfect wow ingredient in a salad or a soup, such as a classic Russian *Rassolnik* (*see* page 95). I am quite excited to share this recipe belonging to my mom, since these fermented cucumbers are legendary among our friends and family. Don't be alarmed by the color of the brine, since it will probably resemble pond water and the pungent smell might take some getting used to. Admittedly, Eastern European ferments are an acquired taste, but if you serve these to some serious ferment connoisseurs, you are likely to get a round of applause.

Line the base of a sterilized 2-liter preserving jar (putting it through a dishwasher on hot should do the job) with some of the celery leaves. Follow with a layer of the whole cucumbers, standing them upright and packing them in tightly, like sardines in a can. Next, add some garlic, chunks of horseradish, a chili half, and half of the dill. Start building the next layer of cucumbers, making sure to leave ½ inch (1 cm) empty at the top of the jar (you might have to trim them slightly to ensure they fit).

To prepare the brine, place the remaining chili half, garlic, and horseradish in a saucepan, add the parsley, fennel, coriander, peppercorns, salt, and distilled water. Bring to boiling point, then turn off the heat and let the mixture infuse as it cools down. Once the infusion has reached room temperature, pour it over the cucumbers, making sure all the chunky bits end up in the jar, too. Finish with a last layer of the remaining celery leaves.

Make sure the cucumbers are fully submerged in brine. You can use a weight to keep them in place—a glass ramekin will do the trick. Close the jar tightly and leave to ferment out of direct sunlight at room temperature for 4–10 days (the speed of fermentation will depend on the temperature in the room). Open the jar daily to let the cucumbers "burp"—you will see the little bubbles starting to rise from the bottom of the jar in about 24 hours.

You will know the cucumbers are ready when the brine starts to darken—hence my comparison to pond water—and they begin to emit a distinct kimchi-like smell. Once you are happy with the degree of fermentation, transfer the jar to the refrigerator. The cucumbers will keep in the cold for a few months, if only you would let them.

Malosolnie Cucumbers

MAKES A HALF-GALLON
(2-LITER) JAR

—

2¼ lb (1 kg) small crunchy
   cucumbers (or larger
   cucumbers cut into batons)
large bunch of dill
4 garlic cloves, peeled
4 celery sticks, cut in half
1 tablespoon black
   peppercorns
1 tablespoon fine salt
4¼ cups (1 liter) good-quality
   sparkling water

Quick-salted (*malosolnie* in Russian) cucumbers are a real treat, and a really lovely way to do something different with the summer glut. But make sure to use the small, sweet, and very crunchy ones to get the best malosolnie experience. These always feature as part of a Russian summer alfresco spread and are usually eaten straight up, with no extra dressing or unnecessary entourage.

Trim the ends of the cucumbers, then place them in a sterilized half-gallon (2-liter) preserving jar (putting it through a dishwasher on hot should do the job) together with the dill, garlic cloves, celery, and peppercorns.

Add the salt to the sparkling water and stir to dissolve, then pour into the jar. Close the jar tightly and refrigerate for a few hours or overnight. The combination of crunchiness, slight fizziness, sharpness, saltiness, and sweetness in this pickle is just so special, and utterly irresistible!

Fermented
Cherry Tomatoes

Officially the best vodka chaser, these fermented tomatoes are sharp, fizzy, tangy, spicy, and refreshing all at once! Knock back a shot, chase it with this little flavor bomb, and you will get the most incredible head rush.

Pack your tomatoes into a sterilized 1.5-liter preserving jar (putting it through a dishwasher on hot should do the job) in layers, interspersed with the garlic cloves, Habanero quarters, dill, and celery leaves.

To prepare the brine, combine the measured water, salt, and peppercorns in a pan and heat to boiling point, then let it cool down completely before adding it to the jar of tomatoes.

Weigh the tomatoes down with a glass ramekin to ensure they are fully submerged in the brine. Close the jar tightly and set aside out of direct sunlight at room temperature for up to a month to ferment. Open the jar every other day to release the gases and to taste the intensity of the flavor. You can transfer the jar to the refrigerator to slow down the fermentation once you are happy with how they taste.

After about 2 weeks, the tomatoes should fall apart inside once you bite into them. Then you know they are ready. They will keep for up to 6 months in the refrigerator.

MAKES A 1½ QUART (1.5-LITER) JAR
(OR USE A LARGER JAR)

—

1¾ lb–2¼ lb (800 g–1 kg)
  cherry tomatoes
6 garlic cloves, peeled
1 Habanero chili pepper,
  quartered
large bunch of dill
large handful of celery leaves
4¼ cups (1 liter) water
1 tablespoon fine salt
1 tablespoon black
  peppercorns

Khrenovina

MAKES A QUART-SIZE (1-LITER) JAR

—

2¼ lb (1 kg) ripe tomatoes

1 tablespoon salt

large chunk of fresh
    horseradish (I would go for
    one the size of two thumbs),
    peeled and finely grated

2 tablespoons clear honey

2 garlic cloves, peeled

This fermented tomato and horseradish salsa might just be my most favorite condiment of all time. Horseradish is a quintessentially Russian ingredient, to such an extent that words deriving from *khren* (Russian for "horseradish") have entered the lexicon to mean things that are completely unrelated to food. The most popular is the adjective *khrenovo*, "horseradish-ish," which means you are not doing too well. Well, I can tell you with all certainty that if you have enough of this wonderful salsa in your diet, things will be anything but *khrenovo* for you. It makes a great salad dressing or condiment for sandwiches; you can add it to your soups for a bit of zing (*see* page 79), or mix it into cocktails (*see* page 226).

Whizz all the ingredients together in a food processor or using a handheld immersion blender.

Transfer to a sterilized quart-size (1-liter) preserving jar (putting it through a dishwasher on hot should do the job), seal tightly, and set aside out of direct sunlight at room temperature for 5–10 days to ferment, depending on the season. Things usually start fermenting a lot faster in the summer. Check on the salsa every day, opening the jar to release the gases. You will know the fermentation has slowed down when there is less gas released from the jar. You will also notice that the salsa might begin to split, with the pulp rising to the top and the clear liquid remaining at the bottom—just give it a good stir when you see that happening. This salsa is very reactive, so you can expect a Champagne cork kind of pop when you open the jar!

Transfer to the refrigerator and enjoy in all the many ways it can be used. It will keep in the fridge for 6 months.

Red Sauerkraut *with* Garlic & Chili

This is a characterful ferment both in looks and flavor. I make it all year round and use it in salads, soups, and stews. You will see several recipes in the book that include this magical ingredient, since the rather pungent but incredibly delicious sauerkraut will bring a real kick to your dishes. Adjust the levels of heat and garlic to your liking, but if you want a sauerkraut that is full of medicinal properties as well as great flavor, I would suggest that you don't be shy with either. It makes a fantastic cure for a cold or a hangover.

Before you do anything, put on some food gloves!

Thinly slice the cabbage into long strips, preferably on a mandolin or using a food processor. Place in a large mixing bowl, add the salt, and massage it into the cabbage quite aggressively for about 5 minutes. This process is quite physically demanding and oddly therapeutic at the same time. You know the cabbage has surrendered when lots of juice comes out and the flesh becomes very soft, yet still crunchy. Add the garlic and chili pepper, and massage for another minute.

Pack the cabbage tightly into a sterilized quart-size (1 liter) preserving jar (putting it through a hot dishwasher should do the job) in layers, making sure there are no air bubbles or gaps as you pack down each layer; you can use a special wooden tamper for fermentation or simply your fist to do this. Continue until the jar is almost full and the cabbage is submerged in its own juice. Weigh it down with a glass ramekin. Make sure you leave a 2 inch (5 cm) gap at the top or the jar will overflow once the process of fermentation begins.

Close the jar tightly and set aside out of direct sunlight at room temperature for 10–14 days so the salt and time can do their magic (naturally, things ferment a lot faster in the summer). It's best to stand the jar inside a bowl in case of spillage. Make sure to check it every day, opening the jar to let the cabbage "burp" or release its gases, and pressing the cabbage down into the brine.

Taste the cabbage after 10 days and leave to ferment for longer if needed. Once you are happy with the taste, transfer the jar to the refrigerator to slow down the fermentation process. It will keep in the fridge for up to 6 months.

MAKES A QUART-SIZE (1-LITER) JAR
—

1 red cabbage, core removed
salt (the desired ratio is
    1 tablespoon salt for every
    2¼ lb/1 kg cabbage, so the
    exact amount depends on
    the weight of your cabbage)
2 garlic cloves, grated
2 teaspoons red pepper flakes
    or 1 small Habanero pepper,
    finely chopped

Apple, Fennel & Dill
Sauerkraut

MAKES A QUART-SIZE (1-LITER) JAR

—

1 white cabbage,
   core removed

1½ tablespoons salt

1 fennel bulb

1 Granny Smith apple

large handful of dill

1 teaspoon toasted
   fennel seeds

The flavor combination of apple, fennel, and dill has to be one of my favorites. I love making a simple green apple and fennel salad, so the idea of creating a sauerkraut using the same blend brought a lot of excitement. Just imagine what will happen to those ingredients once they have undergone the magical process of fermentation. Maximum flavor alert!

This sauerkraut can be consumed on its own with a little drizzle of good-quality unrefined sunflower oil, or add some blood oranges, jalapeños, and dill to turn it into a delicious winter salad.

Remove the outer leaves of the cabbage (reserve one for topping your finished sauerkraut), then cut into quarters and thinly slice using a mandolin or a sharp knife. Place in a large mixing bowl and sprinkle with the salt. Massage the salt into the cabbage for a few minutes and leave to sit while you prepare the rest.

Trim off the root end of the fennel bulb, cut the bulb in half lengthways, and thinly slice lengthways with the mandolin or sharp knife. Next, core and thinly slice the apple. Add to the mixing bowl together with the fennel. The cabbage should have released a lot of juice by this point.

Roughly chop the dill and add it to the bowl, along with the toasted fennel seeds.

Mix everything together thoroughly for about 5 minutes, massaging the cabbage, apples, and fennel to ensure more juices are released.

Finally, pack your sauerkraut mixture tightly into a sterilized quart-size (1-liter) preserving jar (putting it through a dishwasher on hot should do the job) in layers, making sure to get rid of any air pockets or gaps as you pack down each layer, using a special wooden tamper for fermentation or your fist. During this process, more juices will be released and the cabbage should be submerged entirely in its own brine.

Place your reserved cabbage leaf on top of the brine and weigh the sauerkraut down using a glass ramekin. Close the jar tightly and leave to ferment out of direct sunlight at room temperature for 10–14 days, opening to release the gases every other day.

Taste the cabbage after 10 days and leave to ferment for longer if needed. Once you are happy with the taste, transfer the jar to the refrigerator to slow down the fermentation process. It will keep in the fridge for up to 6 months.

Honey Pickled *Daikon*

MAKES A HALF-PINT (250 ML) JAR

—

1 daikon or black radish

⅔ cup (150 ml) water

⅔ cup (150 ml) white wine
   vinegar

4 tablespoons honey

1 tablespoon black
   peppercorns

1 teaspoon red pepper flakes

One of the things that I really appreciate about Russian culinary culture is that food is often used as medicine. There is no profound nutritional knowledge behind this tradition, but rather a reliance on the age-old "grandma and grandpa method," which never fails. We put mustard powder in socks overnight to cure a cold, drink kombucha (or, as it was known in my childhood, "the mushroom") every morning for healthy digestion, and eat a daikon radish–honey concoction to cure a bad cough. While I hated taking any kind of medicine as a kid, I really enjoyed the sweet and fiery cough cure that my mom used to make. So this recipe is a homage to our go-to home potion.

This makes a great addition to a salad, or can be served as part of a vodka and pickles spread.

Peel and thinly slice the daikon or black radish using a mandolin. Place in a sterilized half-pint (250-ml) preserving jar (putting it through a dishwasher on hot should do the job).

Mix together the remaining ingredients in a stainless steel pan. Bring to a boil, then turn off the heat. Make sure the honey has dissolved completely and let the brine infuse until cooled.

Once the brine has reached room temperature, pour over the radish in the jar, close the jar tightly, and refrigerate for 24–48 hours. It will keep for a few months in the refrigerator.

Soviet-Korean Pickles

Whenever I am back in Russia, a trip to the market is never complete without the purchase of some Soviet-Korean pickles. I still get that "kid in a candy store" feeling as I marvel at the variety of choices, from spicy pickled carrots and cabbage (*see* below and opposite) to tofu skins (*see* page 168) and seaweed. Preserved in vinegar, salt, and sugar, with an abundance of garlic and chili, these condiments are inherently Asian, yet over the years they have become a truly "national" food in Russia. So here and in the pages that follow are some recipes for the foods that never fail to seduce me, no matter how much I've consumed in my lifetime.

Carrots

MAKES A PINT-SIZE (500 ML) JAR

—

14 oz (400 g) carrots

1 teaspoon salt

1 onion

2 tablespoons sunflower oil

2 teaspoons Korean Spice Mix
(*see* below)

½ teaspoon cayenne pepper

3 garlic cloves, grated

1 tablespoon sugar

scant ½ cup (100 ml) red wine
vinegar

1 teaspoon white sesame seeds

For the Korean spice mix

2 teaspoons toasted and
freshly ground coriander
seeds (*see* page 31)

1 teaspoon freshly ground
black pepper

1 teaspoon cayenne pepper

½ teaspoon garlic powder

½ teaspoon dried dill

½ teaspoon paprika

½ teaspoon ground bay leaves

To make the spice mix, simply mix all the ingredients together well and store in a small clean airtight jar. Use within 4 months to ensure that the toasted spices don't lose their fragrance.

Peel your carrots, then julienne them into a large non-reactive bowl. Add the salt and massage well into the carrots for a few minutes, then set aside to rest and release their juices. This will take about 30 minutes.

In the meantime, peel and thinly slice the onion, preferably on a mandolin. Heat the oil in a frying pan over medium heat and fry the onion with the 2 teaspoons of your homemade Korean spice mix and the cayenne pepper for 7–10 minutes. Set aside to cool.

While the onion is cooling, you can make the pickling juice. Mix together the garlic, sugar, and vinegar in a non-reactive bowl. Pour the mixture over the carrots and mix in the fried onion and its oil.

To produce the best-tasting result, transfer the carrot mixture to a sterilized pint-size (500 ml) preserving jar (putting it through a dishwasher on hot should do the job), close the jar tightly, and refrigerate overnight, or for at least 2 hours. They will keep in the refrigerator for up to a month.

To serve, all you need to do is sprinkle with the sesame seeds.

Cabbage & Beets

MAKES A QUART-SIZE (1-LITER) JAR

—

1 white cabbage

2 large raw red beets

1 teaspoon salt

1 onion

2 tablespoons sunflower oil

2 teaspoons Korean Spice Mix
(*see* page 166)

½ teaspoon cayenne pepper

3 garlic cloves, grated

1 tablespoon sugar

scant ½ cup (100 ml) red wine
vinegar

Wash and core the cabbage. Cut it into roughly square chunks and set aside in a non-reactive bowl.

Peel the beets and grate or julienne using a julienne peeler (use gloves to avoid staining your hands). Mix with the cabbage.

Add the salt and massage well into the cabbage and beets for a few minutes, then let the vegetables rest to release their juices.

In the meantime, peel and thinly slice the onion, preferably on a mandolin. Heat the oil in a frying pan over medium heat and fry the onion with the Korean spice mix and the cayenne pepper for 7–10 minutes. Set aside to cool.

While the onion is cooling, you can make the pickling juice. Mix together the garlic, sugar, and vinegar in a non-reactive bowl. Pour the mixture over the cabbage and beets and mix in the fried onion and its oil.

To produce the best-tasting result, transfer the carrot mixture to a sterilized quart-size (1 liter) preserving jar (putting it through a dishwasher on hot should do the job), close the jar tightly, and refrigerate overnight, or for at least 2 hours. They will keep in the refrigerator for up to a month.

Pickled Tofu Skins

—

9 oz (250 g) dried tofu skins
  (bean curd sticks or yuba;
  see Suppliers, page 235)

scant ½ cup (100 ml)
  sunflower oil

1 onion, thinly sliced

4 teaspoons toasted and
  freshly ground coriander
  seeds (*see* page 31)

1 teaspoon red pepper flakes

3 tablespoons soy sauce

2 garlic cloves, finely grated

2 tablespoons white wine
  vinegar

1 teaspoon salt

1 teaspoon sugar

I love these tofu skins on their own, or you can throw them into a mixed salad with some grated carrots, cucumbers, sesame oil, and cilantro leaves.

Place the dried tofu skins in a large bowl, pour over boiling water to cover, and let them soak for 2 hours.

Heat the oil in a frying pan over medium heat and fry the onion with the coriander seeds and red pepper flakes for 5 minutes.

Drain the tofu skins and add them to the frying pan, along with the soy sauce. Cook for 1–2 minutes, then turn off the heat and let them cool down.

In the meantime, make the marinade by mixing together the garlic, vinegar, salt, and sugar.

Once the tofu skins are cool, mix them with the marinade and transfer to a storage container with a lid. Cover and refrigerate for a few hours or overnight before serving. They will keep in the refrigerator for up to a month.

Salt & Time

Marinated *Shiitake* Mushrooms

Serve these mushrooms as part of a Korean pickle spread, mix with some cooked cold soba noodles, or add to your mushroom broths for an extra kick!

Place the dried mushrooms in a large non-reactive bowl, pour over the measured boiling water, and let them soak for 30 minutes– 1 hour.

In the meantime, mix all the remaining ingredients together well in a separate non-reactive bowl and let them infuse for a few minutes.

Drain the mushrooms (but reserve the soaking water, since it will make a great base for a rich mushroom broth) and return the mushrooms to the bowl. Pour the marinade mixture over the mushrooms and mix well.

Cover with plastic wrap and refrigerate for at least an hour before serving, but for best results leave to marinate overnight. They will keep in the refrigerator for up to a month.

MAKES A 1 CUP (250 ML) JAR

—

3½ oz (100 g) dried shiitake
   mushrooms
4¼ cups (1 liter) boiling water
1 garlic clove, grated
⅔ cup (150 ml) rice vinegar
6 tablespoons soy sauce
6 tablespoons sesame oil
1 teaspoon Korean Spice Mix
   (*see* page 166)
1 teaspoon salt
½ teaspoon sugar
pinch of red pepper flakes

A New Year's Eve party:
Deviled Eggs with Forshmak
(*see* page 49)
Roast Goose (*see* page 146)
Olivier Salad (*see* page 59)

Desserts

It might be a bit unconventional to open a chapter like this one by confessing that I am not a huge dessert fan—I'm the person who typically orders a cheese board at the end of a meal. However, the very idea of desserts and sweet treats holds a special place in my heart, since for me it is firmly associated with my great-grandma Rosalia. As I have mentioned, she was a trained pastry chef (to our family's delight) and always spoiled both my mom and myself with the most delicious cakes and sweet bakes. I think in my early years I probably ate enough sugary delights to last me for the rest of my life. Rosalia had the most incredible (and difficult) life as a survivor of the Holocaust in Ukraine and an evacuee to Siberia, and I have always longed to share her story. More recently, I realized that cooking is my way of sharing her experience with people and establishing a symbolic connection with her. So this chapter, while not featuring her recipes exclusively, is my celebration of the beautiful, generous, and kind woman that was my great-grandmother Rosalia.

Easter *Paskha* Cheesecake

MAKES 1 CHEESECAKE; SERVES 6–8

—

5¼ tablespoons (2⅔ oz/75 g) unsalted butter, softened

3–4 tablespoons sugar

1 lb (500 g) tvorog (*see page 14*) or farmer cheese or ricotta

5 tablespoons sour cream

1 teaspoon vanilla extract

½ cup (2¾ oz/80 g) toasted almonds, roughly chopped

¾ cup (3½ oz/100 g) mixed dried fruit, such as golden raisins and chopped dried apricots

finely grated zest and juce of ½ lemon

pinch of salt

During the months of February and March, most of Russia becomes vegan for the Great Lent. In a country where you would struggle to find a decent vegetarian dish in most restaurants on any other day of the year, the power of religious convention creates nothing short of a miraculous gastronomic transformation. When I was still too young to make up my own mind about religion, I fasted like the rest of my family. And while I did appreciate the noble purpose of cleansing one's body and soul, what I loved most about Lent was the morning when it was broken! Never a huge fan of meat, I easily gave up my carnivorous habits, but cheese was a true sacrifice. So the thought of tasting my first dairy after 40 days of withdrawal filled me with true joy. This traditional *paskha* cheesecake consumed on Easter morning could not have been more perfect for the occasion if it tried. Made up of nothing but *tvorog*, cream, butter, dried fruits, and nuts, it is a pure dairy epiphany!

Cream the butter and sugar together using a stand mixer fitted with the paddle attachment, or an electric hand mixer, until pale and fluffy. Add the rest of the ingredients and mix until well incorporated and all the dried fruit and nuts are evenly distributed.

Place the mixture in a large piece of cheesecloth, gather the sides of the cloth together to enclose the mixture, and suspend over the sink, in the same way as you would when making labneh (you can do this over a bowl in the fridge, if your kitchen is warm). Leave it there to strain overnight.

The following morning, transfer the mixture to a mold, still keeping it wrapped in the cheesecloth. Traditionally, there are special pyramid-shaped engraved molds that are used for this cheesecake, but you can use any small-medium mixing bowl to achieve a dome-like shape. Press the mixture into the bowl and cover with another piece of cheesecloth. Place a weight on top— you can use a plate and a glass measuring jug filled with water. Leave in the refrigerator for 2–4 hours.

When you are ready to serve the cheesecake, remove the plate and the weight and the top piece of cheesecloth, then pour out any extra liquid that may have been released while it chilled. Turn the bowl over onto a plate and remove the bowl and the remaining cheesecloth.

This cake is served as part of an Easter breakfast spread alongside such lovely things as *kulich* (a Slavic panettone), painted eggs, and pancakes. So if you're not eating it the traditional Slavic way and find that the cheesecake needs a side of carbs, why not crumble some graham crackers on top or serve with a side of grilled sourdough toast drizzled with honey.

Salt & Time

Semolina Cake

Semolina porridge to Soviet kids is like Marmite to the Brits. The entire nation is clearly divided into those who love it and those who hate it, as most of us were force-fed the lumpy substance in kindergarten. I couldn't stand semolina porridge! However, my mom changed my mind when she revamped the notorious porridge into a delicious cake. Very similar to a cornmeal cake, the semolina equivalent is also rich, dense, and textural. I particularly love how the coarse grain offers a lot of bite, while plenty of eggs and butter give it a moist, rich quality. This is a perfect year-round cake that can be eaten at breakfast, as an afternoon treat, or as an after-dinner dessert.

Mix the semolina with the milk or kefir in a bowl, then let it soak for an hour at room temperature.

Preheat the oven to 400°F (200°C). Grease a 9½ inch (24 cm) round cake pan.

Using an electric hand mixer, whisk the eggs, sugar, and butter together in a large mixing bowl until creamy. Add the vanilla extract, baking powder, and salt.

Mix the soaked semolina into the egg mixture, then tip the cake mixture into the greased cake pan. Bake for 40 minutes.

Let the cake cool slightly before serving. You can drizzle some honey or ginger syrup on top to add an extra level of moistness to this wonderfully rich cake. You can serve it with a side of berry coulis or poached fruit and crème fraîche.

MAKES 1 CAKE; SERVES 8–10

—

2¼ cups (13 oz/375 g) semolina

generous 1½ cups (375 ml) milk or kefir

5½ tablespoons (2¾ oz/80 g) unsalted butter, softened, plus extra for greasing

3 eggs

¾ cup (5½ oz/150 g) sugar

1 teaspoon vanilla extract

3 teaspoons baking powder

pinch of salt

clear honey or ginger syrup, for drizzling (optional)

Syrniki Doughnuts

I firmly believe that there exists a secret *babushka* guidebook that states: "Thou shalt overfeed thy grandchildren with *syrniki*." It seems that Russian grannies have an endless supply of these cottage cheese fritters and an understanding that their grandchild has a bottomless stomach that enables them to consume *all* the syrniki on offer. And while I often thought as a child, "I will never lay my eyes on another syrnik ever again," my love of this traditional Russian breakfast-cum-dessert dish has never faltered. Traditionally, syrniki are formed into crumpet-like shapes and fried in a pan. However, at some point back in the early 1990s, when our family acquired a deep-fryer, a new type of syrniki was born—a deep-fried doughnut dusted with sugar. Yes please!

When it comes to accompaniments for these doughnuts, the world is your oyster. Choose anything from yogurt with fruit, to berry jams and compotes, or even dulce de leche.

Using an electric hand mixer, whisk all the ingredients together, except the oil for deep-frying, in a mixing bowl until well incorporated and fluffy. The dough will be very runny, so use a well-floured work surface and 2 tablespoons to shape it into medium-sized doughnut balls. For each doughnut, scoop out a full tablespoon of the dough and roll it around in the flour until it stops sticking to the spoons and the work surface.

Heat the oil for deep-frying in a large pan, keeping it over medium heat to ensure the oil doesn't start to smoke. Test the temperature of the oil by dropping a little of the dough into it—it should start to sizzle but not turn dark brown immediately. Once you are happy with the oil temperature, drop the dough balls in one at a time, making sure they don't stick together. Swirl them around occasionally and remove with a slotted spoon after 1–2 minutes. They should be golden brown and crisp. Lay them out on paper towels and sprinkle with extra sugar.

Serve on a sharing plate with an array of accompaniments for a real feast of a breakfast, or plate them up individually with your accompaniment of choice for an indulgent dessert.

MAKES 10–12

—

7 oz (200 g) tvorog (*see* page 14), or farmer cheese or ricotta

2 eggs

1 tablespoon sugar, plus extra for dusting

½ teaspoon baking powder

pinch of salt

¼ cup (1 oz/30 g) all-purpose flour, plus extra for dusting

2 tablespoons raisins (presoaked in rum or whisky if you'd like to add that extra je ne sais quoi)

finely grated zest of 1 lemon

mild sunflower oil, for deep-frying

Blini *with* Curd & Apricots

SERVES 4

—

For the blini

1⅔ cups (7 oz/200 g) all-
purpose flour

generous ¾ cup (200 ml) milk

3½ tablespoons (1¾ oz/50 g)
unsalted butter, melted, plus
extra for frying and stacking

2 eggs

generous ¾ cup (200 ml)
boiling water

pinch of salt

pinch of sugar

For the filling

7 oz (200 g) goat or cow
cheese curds, or a
scant ½ cup (3½ oz/100 g)
ricotta cheese mixed with a
scant ½ cup (3½ oz/100 g)
cottage cheese

1¼ cups (5½ oz/150 g) ready-
to-eat dried apricots

1 tablespoon sugar,
or to taste

juice of ½ lemon, or to taste

To serve

3½ tablespoons (1¾ oz/50 g)
unsalted butter

1 tablespoon sugar

4 ripe apricots or peaches,
or a mixture of both

sliced almonds, toasted

Before we delve into the recipe, let's take a little linguistic detour. The Russian word *blini* is a plural word referring to crêpes, and what are commonly and technically incorrectly termed "blinis" in the West would be called *oladushki* in Russian. So here I use the word as it was originally intended, for large, thin, buttery crêpes. Blini are an archetypal Slavic dish, dating back to the pagan days when they were prepared to symbolize the sun. The tradition of making blini in spring was then introduced into the Russian Orthodox religion and sustained throughout the atheist Soviet regime.

There are a million and one ways to eat blini: plain with lots of butter, stuffed with dried-fruit jam or sweet *tvorog,* or topped with sour cream and caviar. Stuffed blinis, known in Ashkenazi cuisine as *blintzes*, are my favorite, so here I offer a different stuffing to the traditional sweet tvorog. Make sure to use the plump, juicy type of dried apricots because the really dry ones won't blend well and will just make a lot of noise in your food processor.

To make the blini, sift the flour into a large mixing bowl. Gradually pour in the milk, whisking constantly to make sure there are no lumps, then mix in the melted butter. Break the eggs into the same bowl and whisk until evenly incorporated and a thick batter is formed. Gradually add the measured boiling water and continue whisking until the mixture reaches the right consistency, which should be similar to drinkable yogurt without any lumps. This is a trick I have learned from my grandma, since hot water not only helps to achieve a smooth batter but will also make your blini light and lacy. Season with the salt and sugar.

Heat some butter in a nonstick frying pan over medium-high heat. Pour half a ladle of the batter into the hot pan and swirl it around until it covers the entire surface in an even, paper-thin layer. Cook on one side for about 2 minutes. You know it is ready when the edges start to curl. Flip the crêpe (in the air if you dare) and fry on the other side for 40 seconds or so. Repeat to use up all the batter. Pile the crêpes into a nice stack, adding a thin slice of butter in between every other one.

Blend the cheese curds (or the ricotta and cottage cheese) and dried apricots together in a food processor for 5 minutes or until you have a semi-smooth paste with a few chunky bits, then add the sugar and lemon juice to taste.

To assemble the blintzes, place 2 tablespoons of the cheese mixture on each crêpe and roll into a burrito shape. Heat the butter and sugar together in a frying pan over medium heat. Cut each of the apricots or peaches into 4 slices, removing the pits. Add to the pan and fry for 2–5 minutes until slightly caramelized and softened.

To serve, place 2 blintzes on each plate, add a few of the fried fruit slices, and sprinkle with some toasted sliced almonds.

Salt & Time

Cold Berry Soup

Cold berry soup is a real summer classic in Eastern Europe, from the Baltic countries to Poland and Ukraine, as well as in Russia. A super-simple dish, it consists of any fresh summer berry, milk, and sugar. The best part, of course, is the residue of that sweet, flavored milk at the bottom of the bowl, which holds a very special place in Russian hearts, similar to cereal milk in many Western(-ized) cultures. You can follow the recipe below for a more elaborate version or make your own quick and easy one by just mixing some berries with milk and sugar in a bowl. I honestly can't think of a better breakfast in the summer!

In a small pan, heat the milk with the lemon zest, but don't let it come to a boil.

In the meantime, beat the egg yolk with the sugar in a bowl. Add the warm milk mixture, whisking constantly.

Whizz half of the strawberries in a food processor or a handheld immersion blender until puréed, then add to the milk and egg mixture. Whisk until well incorporated.

Let the mixture cool down and infuse. Once it has cooled to room temperature, strain through a sieve to get rid of any froth and the strawberry seeds.

Cut the rest of the strawberries in half and distribute evenly among 4 bowls. Pour a generous ¾ cup (200 ml) of the strawberry milk into each bowl and decorate with some mint or basil leaves.

SERVES 4

—

3⅓ cups (800 ml) milk

finely grated zest of 1 lemon

1 egg yolk

2 tablespoons sugar

14 oz (400 g) strawberries, hulled, or any summer berry of your choice

a few mint or basil leaves, to decorate

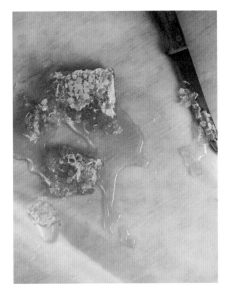

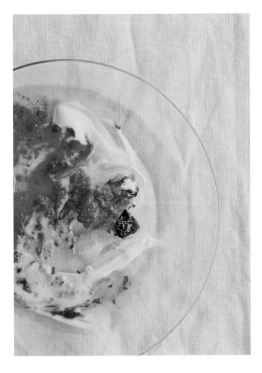

Watermelon Granita *with* Shortbreads

SERVES 4–6

—

For the granita

4½–6½ cups (1½ lb–2¼ lb/ 700 g–1 kg) ripe watermelon pulp

seeds of 1 pomegranate

finely grated zest and juice of 1–2 limes

handful of mint leaves

For the shortbread

(makes about 20)

7 tablespoons (3½ oz/100 g) unsalted butter, softened

¼ cup (1¾ oz/50 g) sugar, plus extra for sprinkling

1¼ cups (5½ oz/150 g) all-purpose flour, plus extra for dusting

prosecco, to serve (optional)

The perks of growing up on the border with Central Asia became most evident in August when all the markets and street kiosks overflowed with watermelons. My Grandpa Yuri was a real expert in selecting a champion watermelon from the gigantic batch. I always loved the sight of watermelons floating in my grandparents' bath; I don't remember the reason, but it had something to do with my grandpa's scientific experiment to demonstrate their excellent quality. One of the other watermelon-related quirks that he had was to enjoy the fruit in question with a slice of white bread. While it may seem rather odd to some, he was not the only person to do so. At one of my recent cinema supper clubs, I showed my favorite Soviet film from the 1980s called *Little Vera*, where one of the characters enjoys exactly the same snack. That scene, as well as my grandpa's eating habit, inspired this recipe for a watermelon granita with a side of buttery shortbread, which I served at the event to rather enthusiastic reviews.

First make the granita. In a food processor, blend together the watermelon pulp, pomegranate seeds, lime zest and juice, and mint leaves until smooth. Pass through a sieve lined with a cheesecloth to get rid of all the seeds and residue.

Pour into a small baking pan, cover with plastic wrap, and put in the freezer for 2–3 hours. Remove from the freezer and scrape the granita with a fork, working from the more frozen edges to the less frozen middle. Re-cover with plastic wrap and return to the freezer for a further 2–3 hours. Repeat 3 or 4 times until the entire tray turns into a frozen-solid crumble.

To make the shortbread, cream the butter and sugar together, using a stand mixer fitted with the paddle attachment or an electric hand mixer, until pale and fluffy. Sift in the flour and mix until the mixture is firm enough to transfer to a lightly floured work surface, then lightly knead into a dough.

Transfer the dough to a sheet of parchment paper and roll out to about ½ inch (1 cm) thick. Place the paper on a baking pan, sprinkle the dough with sugar, then cut into fingers, and refrigerate for 20 minutes to firm up.

In the meantime, preheat the oven to 400°F (200°C).

Remove the pan from the fridge, spread out the fingers on the paper, and bake for 20 minutes until pale golden in color, then let them cool on a wire rack.

To serve, scoop the granita into old-fashioned Champagne glasses (you can drizzle a bit of prosecco on top!) and add the shortbread on the side for a perfect Sunday brunch dessert–cocktail number.

Zephyrs

MAKES ABOUT 80 SMALL,
OR 40 LARGE ZEPHYRS

—

⅔ cup (160 ml) water

⅓ cup (½ oz/15 g) agar flakes

4 egg whites

2¼ cups (1 lb/450 g)
   granulated sugar

confectioner's sugar,
   for dusting

For the raspberry purée

1⅔ cups (14 oz/400 g) frozen
   raspberries

2¼ cups (9 oz/250 g) sugar

When trying to describe *zephyr*, most people refer to it as the love child of a meringue and a marshmallow, and I can't find a more accurate description than that. This beautifully named creation, which is indeed as light as the eponymous wind, has its origin in a medieval Russian dish—an apple and honey *pastila*. Over the centuries eggs were added to the mixture and sugar replaced honey, while the apple flavor remained its signature. Today, zephyr exists in a whole range of pastel colors and flavors, from classic apple to redcurrant, strawberry, and blueberry. So feel free to experiment with colors and flavors and build yourself a show-stopping zephyr tower that would have made Marie Antoinette jealous.

To make the raspberry purée, put the raspberries and sugar in a saucepan over medium heat and cook until they soften and start to break down. Blend thoroughly in a food processor before passing through a sieve. Set aside to cool down.

Pour the measured water into a small saucepan and sprinkle over the agar flakes. Leave to "sponge" for 15 minutes.

When the raspberry purée has cooled to room temperature, transfer it to the bowl of a stand mixer fitted with the whisk attachment, or a large mixing bowl, if using an electric hand mixer. Add the egg whites to the purée and whisk until you have stiff peaks—this can take quite a while, especially if you're using a hand mixer, so be patient. Add the granulated sugar to the agar pan over low heat and stir until dissolved. Next, increase the heat and boil the syrup until it reaches 250°F (120°C) on a candy thermometer.

Immediately pour the syrup in a steady stream into the whipped raspberry mixture while the machine is still running (if using a hand mixer, get someone else to whisk while you pour). Once all the syrup has been poured in, continue to whisk until the mixture is really stiff and holding its shape.

Transfer the mixture to a pastry bag fitted with a star tip and pipe round swirls onto 2 baking sheets lined with parchment paper. Leave to dry out at room temperature for at least 8 hours or overnight.

Stick 2 zephyrs together at the base and dust thoroughly with confectioner's sugar using a sieve. Leave for another few hours for a crisp shell to develop, or enjoy as they are.

Bird *Cherry Cake*

MAKES 1 CAKE; SERVES 8–10

—

For the cake

10½ oz (300 g) bird cherry
 flour (*see* Suppliers,
 page 235)

generous 2 cups (500 ml) milk

2 tablespoons (1 oz/30 g)
 melted butter, plus extra
 for greasing

2¼ cups (9 oz/250 g) sugar

2 eggs

2 teaspoons baking soda

2 cups (9 oz/250 g)
 all-purpose flour

2 tablespoons red wine

For the filling and topping

1½ cups (12 oz/350 g) sour
 cream

¾ cup (5½ oz/150 g) sugar, or
 more if you like it sweeter

Bird cherry trees (*Prunus padus*) blossom all over Russia in late spring. A delicate, fragrant tree, it has inspired a lot of lovely folk and pop songs. In August the tree produces small black berries, similar in appearance to blackcurrants, which are a real staple, particularly in Siberia. Collected in late summer, the berries are used to infuse vodka or are dried out and pounded into a flour. This in turn makes its way into pie fillings and pastry dough. Cakes made from bird cherry flour are characterized by a rich dark color and the most intense tangy, bitter almond and morello cherry-like flavor. A traditional bird cherry cake is served with sweet *smetana* cream and looks dashing in its minimalist black and white attire, and this is exactly what I offer here. If you still have no idea what I am talking about, think of it as a Black Forest Gateau or a Mahlab Cherry Cake Siberian-style.

Mix the bird cherry flour with the milk in a large bowl and let it soak for 1 hour at room temperature.

Preheat the oven to 400°F (200°C). Grease a 9½ inch (24 cm) round cake pan.

Preferably using a stand mixer fitted with the paddle attachment, or if not available, an electric hand mixer, beat the rest of the cake ingredients with the soaked bird cherry flour for a few minutes until you have a smooth mixture.

Pour the batter into the prepared pan and bake for about 40 minutes. Test whether the cake is done by inserting a toothpick into the middle—it should come out dry.

Let the cake cool completely on a wire rack, before carefully slicing it in half horizontally.

To make the filling and topping, beat the sour cream and sugar together in a bowl using an electric hand mixer for 5 minutes until light and fluffy.

Generously smother the bottom half of the cake with some (or all) of the cream mixture and top with the other cake half. You can add another layer of the cream on top or frost the entire cake. I prefer to only put the cream in the middle and to let the monochrome beauty of this cake shine. Refrigerate for a few hours before serving to ensure all the complex flavors have had time enough to mingle. Make sure to play some bird cherry-themed Russian songs as you serve this cake!

Honey Tiramisu

SERVES 4–6

—

5 egg yolks

5 tablespoons clear honey

1 cup (9 oz/250 g) mascarpone

generous 1 cup (9 oz/250 g)
  smetana (*see* page 13) or
  sour cream

generous ¾ cup (200 ml) very
  strong black tea, cooled

7 oz (200 g) ladyfingers,
  preferably without a
  sugar coating

ground cinnamon, for dusting

Before sugar became commonplace in Russia in the 19th century, honey was the ingredient that made life sweeter. Around since the Middle Ages, it was widely used in food and drinks, becoming a key ingredient in defining Russian cuisine. One of the most popular Russian desserts is a cake called *medovik* (from the Russian word for honey, *med*), which was allegedly invented some 200 years ago for the wife of Tsar Alexander I. Consisting of honey-based pastry layers smothered in sweet *smetana* cream, it survived the turbulent course of Russian and Soviet history virtually unchanged.

As much as I love a classic *medovik* cake, I find it a tiny bit too dry for my taste (medovik aficionados, please forgive me). So I've come up with a foolproof, quick-to-make version that borrows the method from my ultimate indulgent dessert—Italian tiramisu. It is abundantly creamy, rich, and light, just like tiramisu, while the flavor of honey and black tea and the tang of smetana never let us forget the Russian origins of this dessert.

Using a stand mixer fitted with the whisk attachment or an electric hand mixer, whisk the egg yolks with the honey for 5–8 minutes until the mixture turns light and fluffy.

Mix the mascarpone and smetana together, then gently fold into the whisked egg yolk mixture.

Pour the tea into a bowl.

Quickly dip each ladyfinger into the tea and arrange in a layer in the base of a medium-sized baking dish, or use individual glasses or bowls. Top with a layer of the honey–smetana mixture, then repeat until you've used up all the ingredients.

Cover with plastic wrap and refrigerate for 3 hours or overnight.

When you are ready to indulge, sprinkle with some cinnamon to add a bit of color and an extra touch of flavor.

Glazed Sandwich Cookies *with* Plum Jam

PICTURED ON PAGES 216–7

MAKES 20–24

—

For the plum jam

2¼ lb (1 kg) ripe, tart plums
   (purple French or Italian
   plums or any dark variety)

1¼ cups (300 ml) cold water

large bunch of tarragon

1¾ lb (800 g) jam or gelling
   sugar (or use granulated
   sugar and one package
   universal pectin; see note)

juice of ½ lemon

pat of unsalted butter

For the cookies

1 stick (4 oz/115 g) unsalted
   butter, softened

generous ½ cup (4 oz/115 g)
   sugar

1 egg

½ teaspoon vanilla extract

2 cups (8½ oz/240 g) all-
   purpose flour

6 tablespoons cornstarch

½ teaspoon salt

For the icing

⅓ cup (3½ oz/100 g) Plum
   Jam (*see* above), plus more
   for spreading

2 cups (8 oz/225 g) sifted
   confectioner's sugar

2–3 tablespoons boiling water

1 teaspoon rose water

202

The official Soviet repertoire of confectionaries was rather limited. If you wanted to treat yourself to some sweet goods from a bakery, cafe, or food shop, you were faced with a line-up of the usual suspects: *zephyr* (*see* page 192), a puff pastry cone with cream, a tartlet with jam and crazy-colored egg white cream, a chocolate "potato"—a simplified version of the Italian chocolate salami—and a bright pink glazed cookie sandwich. The cookie sandwich was my number one choice no matter what. It must have been its shiny pink coating that never failed to attract me. Truth be told, the cookie didn't taste that good, but I hardly knew any better at that age. Luckily, today I have the chance to turn the mundane Soviet creation into something more delicious and appealing. I love cooking with plums and have recently discovered that a combination of tarragon and rose water goes incredibly well with the tart sweetness of the plums. So *voilà*, finally my Soviet childhood delight acquires a more sophisticated flavor profile!

Enjoy these as part of a Russian tea party spread, or just eat them standing in the kitchen with a glass of milk.

To make the jam, pit and quarter the plums. Place in a large pan with the measured water and tarragon and bring to a boil, then simmer over medium heat for 20–30 minutes until the plums are soft and supple and the liquid has reduced.

Add the sugar and lemon juice and stir thoroughly until all the sugar crystals have dissolved and the mixture is no longer grainy. Then boil over high heat for 5–8 minutes.

You can test the jam for its setting point by placing a drop on a chilled saucer. Let the jam cool a little and then push it with your finger. If the jam wrinkles, then it's ready to be put into a jar. If it doesn't, bring back to a boil and cook for a further 2–3 minutes longer, then test again.

Discard the tarragon and stir in the pat of butter. Transfer the jam to a sterilized quart-size (1-liter) jar (putting it through a dishwasher on hot should do the job). Allow to cool fully before closing the jar. This yields more jam than you will need for the recipe, but that's always good news, right?

Salt & Time

The jam will keep in a sterilized airtight container in the refrigerator for up to 6 months. Use within a month once opened.

To make the cookies, line 2 baking sheets with parchment paper.

Cream the butter and sugar together, using a stand mixer fitted with the paddle attachment or an electric hand mixer, until pale and fluffy.

Next, mix in the egg and vanilla extract until well incorporated.

Add the flour, cornstarch, and salt and mix on a medium-low speed. The mixture will look very dry, but keep on beating until bigger clumps are formed and you can easily bring the dough together with your hands.

Roll out the dough between 2 sheets of parchment paper until about ⅛ inch (4 mm) thick, transfer it on the parchment paper to a baking pan, and chill in the refrigerator for 20 minutes to firm up. Preheat the oven to 375°F (190°C).

Remove the dough from the refrigerator. Using a 2 inch (5 cm) cookie cutter, cut out rounds and place on the lined baking sheets.

Bake for 8 minutes until the cookies are cooked but not colored. Remove from the oven and let them cool completely on the baking sheets.

To make the icing, pass the measured jam through a sieve into a bowl, discarding any of the pulp that won't go through the sieve. Mix in the confectioner's sugar until you have a pink ball of dough (it may seem like it won't come together properly but it will!), then gradually stir in the boiling water and the rose water until the mixture is the consistency of thick cream.

To assemble your cookies (if you have kids, this would be really fun for them to do, too!), cover half of the cookie discs with a teaspoon of icing each, and let it set for a few minutes. Place a heaped teaspoon of jam on the remaining cookie discs and then sandwich with the iced cookies.

Note: I use Tate & Lyle Jam Sugar, which already contains pectin (you can find this and other brands of European gelling sugar online). However, if unavailable, use regular granulated sugar with a low- or no-sugar pectin. Follow the package instructions for how much pectin to add, and at what stage, since this varies by brand (some may also require the addition of calcium water).

Carrot & Caraway Cake *with* Smetana

This recipe is one of the few in this chapter that is inspired by one of my favorite childhood sweet treats that I've developed into a more sophisticated dessert suitable for the modern, adult palate. Although there was no shortage of baked cakes and cookies as I grew up, albeit in a limited variety, for some reason I often opted for a "dessert" of grated carrots mixed with sugar and sour cream. Ever since I started planning this book, I wanted to devise a dessert based on this childhood delight. Then one evening I was lucky to be treated to the best dessert I've ever tasted! Rooted in Eastern European flavors, it was created by a dear friend and amazing baker, Henrietta Inman. So this carrot cake is inspired by Henrietta's mesmerizing dessert, and she also kindly helped me develop this recipe.

Preheat the oven to 350°F (180°C). Oil a 9½ inch (24 cm) round loose-bottomed cake pan and line the base with parchment paper.

Mix all the dry ingredients together in a large mixing bowl. In a separate bowl, whisk together the oil, carrots, orange zest, and eggs. Add the wet mixture to the dry mixture and stir well to combine.

Pour the cake mixture into the prepared pan and bake for about 40 minutes until dark brown on top.

Let the cake cool slightly before serving. Enjoy with a big dollop of smetana or sour cream! I prefer mine plain, but you can always add some sugar, honey, or orange zest to yours if you like.

MAKES 1 CAKE; SERVES 8–10

—

1¾ cups (8 oz/225 g) all-purpose flour

⅔ cup (4½ oz/125 g) organic cane sugar

1 loose cup (4¾ oz/135 g) soft dark brown sugar

1 teaspoon baking powder

1 teaspoon baking soda

½ teaspoon ground allspice

2 teaspoons toasted caraway seeds

½ teaspoon sea salt flakes

¾ cup (3¼ oz/90 g) roughly chopped toasted walnuts

scant ½ cup (100 ml) good-quality unrefined sunflower oil, plus extra for greasing

1 ¾ cups (7 oz/200 g) grated peeled carrots

finely grated zest of 1 orange

3 eggs

To serve (optional)
smetana or sour cream
clear honey or sugar
finely grated orange zest

Pine Nut
& Honey Cake

An indisputable family favorite, this simple-looking but mighty-tasting cake has graced the festive table on a number of occasions: from most of the winter holidays to Easter weekend, and on occasional lazy Sundays. Made up of pretty much nothing else but honey, butter, and pine nuts, to me this cake encapsulates the key flavors of Siberia (the land of honey and pine nuts!). Aside from its buttery richness and the slightly bitter crunch of the pine nuts, what I love about this cake is its versatility; add some orange or lemon zest, drizzle with olive oil, and decorate it with rosemary, and your classic Siberian cake turns into a luscious Mediterranean treat.

Preheat the oven to 350°F (180°C).

Spread the pine nuts out on a large baking sheet and toast in the oven for a few minutes until golden brown, stirring occasionally. Set aside to cool.

Increase the oven temperature to 400°F (200°C). Grease a 9½ inch (24 cm) cake pan.

Cream the butter and sugar together, using a stand mixer fitted with the paddle attachment or an electric hand mixer, until pale and fluffy.

Add the eggs, one at a time, while you continue to mix on a lower speed. Then mix in the honey and fold in the toasted pine nuts, reserving a handful.

Pour the cake mixture into the prepared pan, sprinkle the remaining pine nuts on top, and bake for 30 minutes, or until a toothpick inserted into the middle comes out clean.

Let the cake cool on a wire rack and serve with an extra drizzle of honey or a dusting of confectioner's sugar.

MAKES 1 CAKE; SERVES 8–10
—
scant 2 cups (9 oz/250 g)
   pine nuts
2¼ sticks (9 oz/250 g)
   unsalted butter, softened,
   plus extra for greasing
1 cup (7 oz/200 g) sugar
3 eggs
¼ cup (3 oz/85 g) clear honey,
   plus extra to serve (optional)
scant 1 cup (4 oz/115 g) all-
   purpose flour
confectioner's sugar, for
   dusting (optional)

Rye Bread &
Butter Pudding

SERVES 8

—

unsalted butter, enough to
   butter each slice and grease
   the baking dish
16 slices of Russian rye bread
1 cup (5½ oz/150 g) roughly
   chopped dried sour cherries
   or whole golden raisins
2 teaspoons ground pumpkin
   pie spice
2½ cups (600 ml) milk
generous ¾ cup (200 ml)
   heavy cream
2 bay leaves
1 teaspoon toasted coriander
   seeds (see page 31)
8 egg yolks
¾ loose cup (3½ oz/100 g)
   brown sugar, plus a few
   pinches for dusting

A lot of my early childhood memories feature my maternal grandparents' kitchen: the tiny space in their Soviet one-room apartment with a wooden table in the middle and a red lampshade hanging over it. That was the stage for some very special moments, from playing my favorite "train game" with my grandpa (the premise could not be simpler—we would be having tea while pretending to be in a train compartment), to gobbling up the food prepared by my grandma. One particular food-related memory has stuck with me until this day. I can see myself so clearly at that table under the red lampshade eating a slice of buttered rye bread with sugar. The idea for it came after watching an episode of the popular Soviet TV series *The Meeting Place Cannot Be Changed*, where the charismatic protagonist makes himself that very snack. Set in the post-World War II Soviet Union, the show gave good insight into the rather dreary gastronomic realities of the 1950s. A contemporary of that era, my grandma was surprised at my eagerness for the sugary slice of bread, since to her it was a symbol of the hard years. I had not revisited this snack for decades, but its flavor came back to me while brainstorming recipes for this chapter. Taking inspiration from a classic bread pudding, I've made this Sovietized version, which marries the two strands of my culinary identity so well.

This dessert is pretty rich and warming, so you may want to serve it after a light meal. But then, I would never stop you from over-indulging.

Grease a medium-sized ovenproof dish. Remove the crusts from the slices of bread (make sure to keep them, since they will come in handy when making Kvass, *see* page 222). Generously butter each slice and arrange 8 slices on the base of the dish, making sure they fit as snugly as possible. Add a layer of dried sour cherries or raisins. Sprinkle with 1 teaspoon of the pumpkin pie spice, and cover with another layer of bread (you can stand this layer up as pictured, if you like). Set aside while you prepare the custard.

Heat the milk, cream, bay leaves, and coriander seeds in a saucepan. Do keep an eye on it, since you don't want the milk and cream to boil. As soon as the mixture reaches boiling point, turn off the heat and leave it to infuse for 30 minutes. Then strain through a sieve to remove the bay leaves and coriander seeds.

Beat the egg yolks with the sugar in a large bowl until well combined. Then add your infused milk and mix well.

Pour the custard over the bread, sprinkle with the remaining teaspoon of spice and the extra sugar, and let the bread pudding rest for 30 minutes at room temperature. Preheat the oven to 350°F (180°C).

Bake for 30 minutes, until the custard has set. Serve immediately.

Prune &
Walnut Brownies

SERVES 8–12

—

2¼ sticks (9 oz/250 g)
   unsalted butter
7 oz (200 g) dark chocolate
   (80% cocoa solids),
   broken up
1 cup (2¾ oz/80 g)
   unsweetened cocoa powder
½ cup (2 oz/60 g) all-purpose
   flour
1½ cups (10½ oz/300 g) sugar
1 teaspoon baking powder
scant ½ cup (2¾ oz/80 g)
   pitted prunes, roughly
   chopped
½ cup (2 oz/60 g) roughly
   chopped walnuts
4 eggs
whipped smetana (see
   page 13), plain yogurt, or
   sour cream, to serve

Prunes and walnuts are widely used in Russian cuisine. They contribute a very distinct character in both flavor and texture, whether added to sweet or savory dishes. They are most popular in a beet salad with garlic and mayo, or as a sweet snack of prunes stuffed with walnuts, either coated in chocolate or smothered in sweet *smetana*. As you have probably guessed by now, I love adding traditional Russian flavors to my favorite dishes from other countries. So here is another recipe that infuses a Western dessert with an Eastern accent. You just can't go wrong when spiking a chocolate brownie with the smoky tang of prunes, the rich crunch of walnuts, and the light, almost savory creaminess of smetana.

Preheat the oven to 400°F (200°C). Line a 6 by 9 inch (15 by 23 cm) brownie pan or dish with parchment paper. (You can also use an 8 inch/20 cm round cake pan.)

Melt the butter and chocolate together in a heatproof bowl set over a pan of barely simmering water.

In a separate bowl, mix together the cocoa, flour, sugar, baking powder, prunes, and walnuts. Pour the hot butter and chocolate mixture into the dry ingredients and mix together thoroughly until evenly combined.

Beat the eggs together in another bowl and then add to the bowl with the brownie mixture. At first they might not want to integrate, but keep mixing for 2–3 minutes and you will soon get an even and silky batter.

Pour the brownie batter into the prepared pan and shake the pan to ensure the batter spreads in an even layer.

Bake for 20–25 minutes until the edges of the brownie are set, while the middle remains gooey.

Let the brownie cool completely in the pan (it might crumble apart otherwise).

Cut into slices and serve each slice with a generous dollop of whipped smetana, yogurt, or sour cream.

Napoleon Cake

SERVES 8–10

—

For the pastry
6 cups (1 lb 10½ oz/750 g)
    all-purpose flour, plus
    extra for dusting
2¼ sticks (9 oz/250 g) very
    cold unsalted butter
1 egg
1 teaspoon white wine vinegar
small pinch of salt
about ⅔ cup (150 ml) very cold
    water

For the crème pâtissière
4 egg yolks
2 cups (14 oz/400 g) sugar
generous 2 cups (500 ml) milk
2 teaspoons all-purpose flour
2 teaspoons cornstarch
4 sticks (1 lb/500 g) unsalted
    butter, softened
2 teaspoons vanilla extract

This cake is the royalty of Soviet desserts. A relative of the French *millefeuille*, the Napoleon cake was invented in 1912 to celebrate the centenary of Russia's victory over the invading Napoleonic army. Characterized by numerous layers of buttery pastry and rich vanilla crème pâtissière, the cake was simplified during the Soviet era and became a real icon of any celebration, be it New Year's Eve or a birthday party. In my family, naturally my great-grandma Rosalia (born the same year as the cake) made the best Napoleon. And for me, her memory is alive whenever I taste that buttery vanilla custard and flaky pastry combo. This is her signature recipe.

To make the pastry, pulse the flour and butter together in a food processor until you have uniform crumbs with no lumps of butter within the flour. Transfer the mixture to a bowl. In a separate bowl, beat the egg, vinegar, and salt together, then stir into the crumbed mixture, incorporating it quickly and thoroughly. Add enough of the measured cold water for the mixture to come together and form a ball, then knead together until you have a workable dough.

Divide the pastry dough into 8 equal parts, wrap each part in plastic, and refrigerate for a few hours until firm. Preheat the oven to 425°F (220°C).

Roll out each portion of pastry on a lightly floured work surface into an even circle, about 9½ inch (24 cm) in diameter, and as thin as a French crêpe. Transfer to a baking pan and prick with a fork in a few places to prevent bubbles from forming. Bake each for about 10 minutes until the pastry starts to brown. Cool on a wire rack.

To make the custard, mix together the egg yolks, sugar, milk, flour, and cornstarch in a saucepan. Stirring constantly, bring the mixture to a boil, then take off the heat and let cool slightly. Beat in the butter, a few tablespoons at a time to avoid lumps forming, along with the vanilla extract. You may need to return the pan to low heat if you notice that the custard is cooling down too much.

To assemble, generously smother each layer of pastry with the custard and stack them up. Set one pastry layer aside and, once all the other layers are in place, crumble it on top of the cake to resemble the snow that sealed the fate of Napoleon and his army back in 1812. Let the cake rest in the refrigerator overnight and enjoy as many slices as you physically can!

An afternoon tea party.
Glazed Sandwich Cookies
with Plum Jam (*see* pages
202–3)
Pine Nut and Honey Cake
(*see* page 207)
Zephyrs (*see* page 192)
Carrot and Caraway Cake with
Smetana (*see* page 205)

Drinks

Chapter 6

Oh, where do I begin! As I said in the introduction to this book, I want to move away from the stereotypes of Russia, incessant vodka drinking being one of them, but at the same time we can't deny this tradition entirely. Russians do like to drink, and vodka is of course a big part of the gastronomic identity. The word "vodka" originates from the Slavic *voda*, which means "water"; and just like the French *eau de vie* (brandy) or Gaelic *uisce beatha* (whiskey), the spirit is appreciated as a vital part of our culture and diet. So I see this love for "the water of life" as a unifying factor, which is shared by so many cultures where drinking is inextricably linked to the way we eat. You have probably guessed that I do like my vodka and other alcoholic beverages, given that vodka was the first thing to come to mind when writing this very introduction. But worry not; in this chapter I will share a range of drinks: soft drinks, non-alcoholic fermented drinks, and hot infusions and teas, besides both new and traditional vodka infusions and other boozy cocktails.

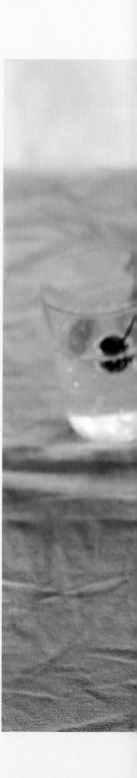

220

Summer Berry *Kissel*

Any drink that has the word "kiss" in its name promises to be a delightful one! *Kissel* is a curious creature—a cross between a jelly and a juice. At Soviet kindergarten it was given to us to drink or eat with a spoon after lunch: tart, sweet, and slightly chewy, it was as nutritious as it was fun to consume.

Mash the berries in a bowl with a spoon and then pass through a fine sieve, reserving the purée for later.

Place the berry pulp and skins left in the sieve in a saucepan with the measured water and sugar. Bring to a boil, stirring until the sugar has dissolved, then reduce the heat and simmer for 5–10 minutes.

Strain the hot infusion through a sieve, discarding the solids, and return the liquid to the pan.

Mix the potato starch with ½ cup (120 ml) water in a bowl until the starch has dissolved. Bring the berry infusion back to a boil, then reduce the heat and gradually pour in the starch solution, stirring constantly. Cook for 5 minutes, continuing to stir. Add the berry purée and give the mixture a last good stir.

Turn off the heat and let it cool completely before drinking within 2–4 days.

MAKES 4¼ CUPS (1 LITER)

—

1¾ cups (9 oz/250 g) berries (use any variety you like)
4¼ cups (1 liter) water
3–4 tablespoons sugar (the amount will depend on how tart the berries are)
2 tablespoons potato starch

Silver Birch Tears

The silver birch is considered to be a quintessential Russian tree. A symbol of femininity in national folklore, silver birches "cry" on the cusp of spring, which is a rather captivating sight. The sap that comes out from underneath the bark can be collected in jars and enjoyed as a juice.

Put the lemon quarter, lemon thyme, and mint in a large mixing glass and pound with a cocktail muddler or the end of a rolling pin until all the juice is released from the lemon. Remove the lemon skin. Add the vodka and silver birch juice and stir well.

Pour into a short glass with some ice and top up with a splash of soda water. Decorate with lemon peel and lemon thyme.

SERVES 1

—

¼ lemon
small bunch of lemon thyme, plus extra to serve
handful of mint leaves
1⅔ tablespoons vodka
scant ½ cup (100 ml) silver birch juice (*see* Suppliers, page 235)
splash of soda water
pared lemon, to serve

Kvass

—

7 oz (200 g) rye bread crusts

8½ cups (2 liters) warm water

¼ cup (1¾ oz/50 g) sugar,
   plus extra to taste

4 teaspoons (½ oz/15 g)
   instant yeast

1 tablespoon raisins

2–4 tablespoons clear honey

2 slices peeled fresh ginger
   (optional)

2 lemon slices (optional)

"Her name was Larisa. She was a *kvass* girl." Thus began an autobiographical account that my mom's school friend wrote about her summer vacation. This opening line has stuck with me for years, not only because there is something Hemingway-esque about its simplicity but also because it so vividly evokes the nostalgic image of that iconic two-wheeled yellow cistern filled with kvass. Sprouting up around the city every summer, each cistern had a kvass vendor, like Larissa, a long line of customers and—dare I say it—one glass for communal use. While today kvass is becoming increasingly trendy in the West, along with kombucha and sauerkraut, this fermented rye bread drink has been around in Russia since the Middle Ages and continues to enjoy wide popularity in the post-Soviet era, where it is produced on a mass scale in giant plastic bottles in a rather overtly nationalistic attempt to compete with the popularity of Western sugary drinks. Never a fan of drinks that come in plastic bottles with a patriotic message, I love making my own kvass and experimenting with different flavor combinations.

Place the crusts in a sterilized half-gallon (2-liter) preserving jar (putting it through a dishwasher on hot should do the job). Mix the measured warm water with the sugar in a bowl or pan until the sugar has dissolved. Pour over the crusts in the jar and soak for 30–40 minutes. Pour out a generous ¾ cup (200 ml) of the water from the jar into a jug, add the yeast, and stir to dissolve. Keep in a warm place until the mixture starts to bubble.

Tip the yeast mixture into the jar with the bread and close the lid, removing the rubber seal, or cover with only a piece of cheesecloth (I cover it with a food glove, which inflates, indicating fermentation is underway, but this is not necessary). Leave to ferment at room temperature for 48 hours.

Strain the contents of the jar through a cheesecloth and transfer to another sterilized half-gallon (2-liter) jar, adding the raisins and more sugar to taste. Leave to ferment for another day before straining it again, then pouring into a sterilized half-gallon (2-liter) jar or glass bottle. At this point you need to add the honey and some extra elements, such as the ginger or lemon (or both). Place in the refrigerator to slow down the fermentation process and get ready to enjoy a glass of cold, fizzy, and pungent kvass the next day. It will keep in the refrigerator for up to 2 weeks.

Salt & Time

224

Sea Buckthorn *Mors*

If I were to choose one word to define the taste of my childhood, it would without a doubt be my Siberian compatriot *oblepikha*, or sea buckthorn (*see* page 13). Obsessed with its bright orange color and sweet yet tangy flavor (a peculiar mix of mango, orange, peach, and honeysuckle), I would eat *oblepikha* every single day. Luckily my grandma had a lifelong supply of the berry in various guises, from jam (yes please, with a stack of pancakes) to frozen berries that turned into the most delightful *mors* drink. Mors is a term used for a hot or cold drink made by mixing puréed berries with a sweet berry stock. It has a really delightful intensity of flavor and a unique consistency. Purée the berries with the sugar alone and you will get a wonderful quick raw jam, or add them to vodka to create your own homemade infusion (*see* pages 231–4).

Rinse the berries and blend them in a food processor with 1 tablespoon of the sugar. Pass through a sieve or a piece of cheesecloth until you have a runny purée (you have your raw jam at this point).

To make the mors, set the purée aside and place what's left in the sieve into a saucepan with the measured water and the remaining 2 tablespoons of sugar. Bring to a boil, then reduce the heat and simmer gently for 15 minutes. Turn off the heat and let the mixture infuse for 30 minutes.

Strain the infusion through a sieve into a bowl, then stir it into the berry purée to achieve that distinct mors consistency.

The mors can be enjoyed hot or cool, depending on the season, but is best consumed within 2–4 days of making. Add a shot of vodka, or top with some bubbly with a few ice cubes, to make yourself a rather delicious cocktail.

MAKES 6⅓ CUPS (1.5 LITERS)

—

14 oz (400 g) fresh or frozen sea buckthorn berries (*see* Suppliers, page 235)
3 tablespoons sugar
6⅓ cups (1.5 liters) water

Bloody Masha

SERVES 1 (DOUBLE SHOT)
—

1 cup (250 ml) good-quality
    tomato juice
3½ tablespoons Horseradish,
    Honey & Chili Vodka (*see*
    page 231) or plain vodka
3½ tablespoons Khrenovina
    (*see* page 158) or any
    fermentation liquid
4 dashes of Worcestershire
    sauce
4 dashes of Tabasco sauce
juice of ½ lemon
large pinch of sea salt flakes
grind of black pepper

To decorate
1 celery stick
1 slice of Fermented Cucumber
    (*see* page 152
    for homemade)

A man walks into his kitchen wearing a pair of boxer shorts. He opens the fridge, takes out a jar of ferments, and drinks the brine straight from it. This is what a hangover looks like in a Soviet mind's eye. Indeed, while here in the West we'd opt for a Bloody Mary, the hungover folk back in the USSR would reach for that brine. So this recipe mixes the best of both cures.

Mix all the main ingredients together in a cocktail shaker or a mixing glass.

Pour into a cocktail glass and top with ice.

To decorate, add a celery stick and a slice of fermented cucumber. Alternatively, this drink can be consumed from a large jar while wearing boxer shorts if you would like to enhance the "Soviet" experience.

Medok

PICTURED OPPOSITE
SERVES 1
—

generous ¾ cup (200 ml) hot
    water
2 teaspoons honey
2 tablespoons applesauce
4 thyme sprigs, plus an extra
    sprig to decorate
1 apple slice, to decorate

This recipe has its roots in a canteen in Sochi. When my family holidayed at this seaside town in 1986, we would frequent a dumplings canteen that served a sweet honey drink called *medok*. It was love at first sip! This is my more sophisticated version, of course.

Put all the ingredients in a cup and infuse for a few minutes.

To serve, decorate with an additional thyme sprig and an apple slice. I can't help but note that you can create a wonderful party cocktail too, if you let the drink cool down completely, add lots of ice and a shot of vodka.

Persimmon Bellini

PICTURED OPPOSITE

SERVES 4

—

2 very ripe persimmons,
    roughly chopped

1 tablespoon sugar

juice of ½ lemon

⅔ cup (150 ml) water

750 ml bottle of sparkling wine
    or Champagne

4 persimmon slices,
    to decorate

I associate persimmon with my great-grandma Rosalia. Born in Ukraine, she spent her adulthood in Siberia missing the abundance of fruit she had in her childhood. She often reminisced about her persimmons and I could not wait to give them a try. While my first experience of an under-ripe persimmon was disappointing to say the least, over the years, ripe persimmons and I became good friends. The older I grew the more I understood Rosalia's love for this utterly unique fruit.

Blend the persimmons with the sugar, lemon juice, and measured water in a food processor. Strain through a sieve to obtain a silky smooth purée.

Add a tablespoon of the purée to each glass (I would recommend using old-fashioned Champagne coupes) and top each with a generous ¾ cup (200 ml) of the bubbly. Give it a gentle stir, decorate with a persimmon slice, and enjoy immediately!

Sbiten

MAKES A 2-LITER JAR

—

⅔ cup (150 ml) honey

⅔ cup (7 oz/200 g)
    blackcurrant or plum jam
    (*see* page 202)

1 tablespoon cloves

2 cinnamon sticks

1 teaspoon ground ginger

½ teaspoon red pepper flakes

¼ teaspoon ground nutmeg

8½ cups (2 liters) water

Move over hot spiced wine, here comes Russian *sbiten*. The most popular drink from ancient days through the 19th century, this honey-and-spice infusion is enjoying a bit of a comeback. Substitute water for red wine and you are all set for the festive season.

Put all the ingredients in a saucepan and bring to a boil over medium heat, stirring occasionally. Don't let the liquid boil vigorously, and take off the heat as soon as bubbles start to appear. Let the mixture cool to room temperature and infuse.

Strain through a piece of cheesecloth or a fine sieve and consume straight away, or transfer to a sterilized glass bottle (putting it through a dishwasher on hot should do the job) and keep refrigerated for up to a week. It tastes equally good hot or cold, but a hot cup of sbiten can't be beaten on a cold winter evening.

Siberian Tea Blend

Makes about 1 lb (500 g)

—

2½ oz (70 g) dried
    meadowsweet (leaves and
    blossoms)

1¾ oz (50 g) pieces of dried
    Rhodiola rosea root

1¾ oz (50 g) pieces of Siberian
    ginseng (or use Chinese
    white ginseng)

2½ oz (70 g) dried redcurrant
    leaves (if available)

3½ oz (100 g) dried rosehips

1¾ oz (50 g) dried oregano
    flowers

3½ oz (100 g) black or green
    loose-leaf tea

Despite living in the coldest part of the country, Siberians are generally considered to have the best health among all Russians and it is common to wish someone "Siberian health." Back in the Soviet days, most major pharmacies had a natural remedy section where one could enjoy a cup of herbal tea, a vitamin cocktail, or a special hot infusion, depending on their ailment. I loved visiting my local pharmacy when I was little, not only to enjoy their drinks but also to marvel at the old wooden counter and the dark apothecary jars inside glass cabinets. It was such an alluring, magical space. Today, Siberian herbs are enjoying a revival, and dedicated stores and market stalls are popping up all over the country. So here is a blend of the most popular Siberian herbs and berries, which are also available in the West (*see* Suppliers, page 235).

Mix all the ingredients together in an airtight jar; this will keep for months.

    To make the tea, add a tablespoon of the blend per cup, or 2–3 tablespoons for a pot of tea. Pour over boiling water and leave to brew for 10 minutes, then enjoy your hot cup of Siberian tea.

Vodka Infusions

What I love most about drinking vodka is that it turns a meal into a ritual. If you decide to drink vodka with your dinner, you can't just put any old meal on the table. The drink dictates your menu!

Infusing vodka is a great way to add flavor to the fiery liquid and to make the food pairings all the more exciting.

Dark Berry Vodka

MAKES A QUART-SIZE (1-LITER)
JAR OR BOTTLE

—

2½ cups (12 oz/350 g) dark berries, such as blackberries or blackcurrants
2 bay leaves
1 tablespoon black peppercorns
½ cup (3½ oz/100 g) sugar
3 cups (750 ml) good-quality vodka

This has to be the most dangerous infusion, so pleasant on the palate that you forget you are drinking vodka.

Put all the flavorings and sugar in a sterilized quart-size (1-liter) preserving jar or glass bottle (putting it through a dishwasher on hot should do the job), top with the vodka, and close tightly, then let the infusion begin by placing it in a dark place at room temperature.

The vodka can be consumed as early as after a month but, as with all vodka infusions, if you let time work its magic, you will be rewarded with some incredible flavor. And take just a bite of that boozy berry—it will really add an extra perk to the whole experience.

Horseradish, Honey & Chili Vodka

MAKES A QUART-SIZE (1-LITER)
JAR OR BOTTLE

—

1 fresh horseradish root, peeled and roughly chopped
1 dried chili pepper (the size depends on your personal taste for heat)
1 tablespoon clear honey
2 teaspoons black peppercorns
pared zest of ½ lemon
3 cups (750 ml) vodka

This pairs beautifully with any dish containing ferments, and can be enjoyed before a meal to ignite the appetite. Make sure to use good-quality vodka.

Put all the flavorings in a sterilized quart-size (1-liter) preserving jar or glass bottle (putting it through a dishwasher on hot should do the job), top with the vodka, and close tightly. Leave to infuse in a dark place at room temperature for a minimum of a month. The longer the infusion time, the better the flavor.

Pine Nut Vodka

Siberia, with its abundance of pine forests, is the homeland of the most fragrant and plump pine nuts. Easily affordable in Siberia while considered a delicacy across Russia, pine nuts are sold unshelled in big bags and were consumed in our household by the kilogram. High in nutrients and flavor, their shells make a perfect foundation for this vodka infusion. Leave them to soak for a minimum of six months until they lose their color and turn the vodka into a beautiful dark elixir. If you struggle to find unshelled pine nuts, try using unshelled walnuts instead.

Put the pine nuts (or walnuts) and sugar in a sterilized quart-size (1-liter) preserving jar or glass bottle (putting it through a dishwasher on hot should do the job), top with the vodka, and close tightly. Store in a dark place at room temperature for at least 6 months. This infusion makes a wonderful digestif!

MAKES A QUART-SIZE (1-LITER)
JAR OR BOTTLE

—

10½ oz (300 g) unshelled pine nuts (*see* Suppliers, page 235), or unshelled walnuts

2 tablespoons sugar

3 cups (750 ml) good-quality vodka

Christmas Vodka

This is an entirely made-up infusion that is not traditional in Russia, but rather uses the scents and colors we associate with Christmas here in the West. As you have guessed by now, vodka is a wonderful foundation for creating your own bespoke infusions, so go ahead and let your imagination wander.

Put all the flavorings and sugar in a sterilized quart-size (1-liter) preserving jar or glass bottle (putting it through a dishwasher on hot should do the job), top with the vodka, and close tightly.

Leave to infuse in a dark place at room temperature for a minimum of a month. The longer the infusion time, the better the flavor. This jar or bottle of infused vodka will keep unopened for years but will vanish in the blink of an eye once opened.

MAKES A QUART-SIZE (1-LITER)
JAR OR BOTTLE

—

seeds of 1 pomegranate

pared zest of 1 orange

2 cinnamon sticks

1 teaspoon cloves

1 teaspoon black peppercorns

3 cardamon pods

½ cup (3½ oz/100 g) sugar

3 cups (750 ml) good-quality vodka

Salt & Time

Suppliers

For Siberian pine nuts and bird cherry flour
www.siberiangreenfood.com
www.siberiantreasure.ru (also sold on Amazon,
or check Eastern European food stores)

For ingredients for Siberian tea and many of the
spices, seeds, and grains mentioned throughout
the book, visit Kalustyan's
123 Lexington Avenue, New York, NY 10016
www.foodsofnations.com

For roasted buckwheat (*kasha*)
www.bobsredmill.com (also sold in many
grocery stores)

For specialist ingredients such as tvorog,
herring, kvass, smetana, roasted buckwheat,
Georgian Suluguni cheese, Russian rye and
Borodinsky bread, and organic raw sunflower oil
www.russiantable.com
www.russianfoodusa.com

Look for silver birch juice in natural food stores
or online at www.sapplife.co

Look for fresh sorrel and fresh fiddlehead ferns
in farmers' markets and specialty grocery stores
in late spring, or ask an experienced forager
to help you pick some. For brined ferns, check
online or your local East Asian grocery stores.

Look for tofu skins (also called bean curd
sticks, yuba, or soybean skin) in East Asian
grocery stores.

For sea buckthorn
www.nwwildfoods.com

Index

Index

Thank You

Stephanie Jackson your passion for my work made me believe that my story is worth telling. I am beyond grateful that you have made me feel so welcomed into the Octopus family and allowed me so much creative freedom in making this book.

Zoe Ross you are an absolute dream of an agent! Our first meeting and subsequent work on the proposal happened at a very difficult time, but your enthusiasm for my idea and your insightful guidance were key to making this book happen.

Juliette Norsworthy and Pauline Bache I absolutely loved working with you! Thank you for translating my ideas so sensitively and for being so generous with your time and guidance.

Lizzie Mayson I am so lucky to have come across a photographer who not only shared my vision but also the love of Russian food, culture, and landscape. We've create a book that is far better than I could have imagined.

Tamara Vos and Louie Waller I fell in love with your style at first Insta-sight! I am so happy that you were part of this project and graced this book with your unique touch.

Charlotte Heal your work brought all the words and images together in the most elegant and harmonious way and that's when the book was really born! Thank you to all the assistants on the UK shoot— Stephanie McLeod, Shambala Fisher, and Sophie Pryn, especially, who shared her culinary talent when it came to developing some of the dessert and pastry recipes. Sophie, you are officially the queen of zephyrs!

Olia Hercules thank you for your friendship and for inspiring me to pursue my passion. Your role in making this book a reality is immense, and your amazing food and your kindness will always have a very special place in my heart!

Joe Woodhouse thank you for your advice and guidance throughout the making of the book proposal! And for inspiring me to be a more adventurous cook when it comes to veggies!

Alexie Kharibian and Dom Millard cooking with you was such an exciting beginning of my culinary journey. Thank you for having me over at your lovely cafe, which was where I hosted my very first Russian supper club!

Sanaz Zardoscht you are an amazing chef and I am so grateful for everything I have learned while working with you!

Romy Gill for inviting me to take part in the first Severn Sisters dinner! I didn't know it then but it was a first step towards creating this book.

Henrietta Inman thank you for sharing your recipe in this book and for inspiring me to be a more brave and adventurous baker.

KinoVino guest chefs you have been the most amazing teachers one could dream of. Thank you for being part of my supper club and for encouraging me to pursue my own cooking!

Mehmet Aksoy it breaks my heart knowing that you will never see this book. But your tragic, untimely death played an important part in making it happen. It was a painful and powerful reminder that, just like you, I should always be true to myself.

To the recipe testers, Sharon and Pamela Browell, Janet Mackechnie, Jack Martin, Claudia Prieto, and Boris and Svetlana Boiko, for your enthusiasm about my food! Your feedback and suggestions were absolutely invaluable and have saved me from making some really silly mistakes!

Helen Osgerby of Simple Shape thank you for lending me some of your exquisite ceramics!

Holly Allenby of ACEY thank you for lending me the most gorgeous outfits.

WORM London thank you for the stunning florals; I wish I could feature them on every page!

My mama, Olga, and papa, Dmitri, for encouraging and supporting me in whatever I do! To my mom especially, for all the cooking classes at home over the years and for your help with this book!

Ksenia Vashchenko for being the most amazing friend and partner in all sorts of crimes, for your enthusiasm about my cooking, and your incredible input into KinoVino events.

Steve Browell all of this would not have been possible without you! You've been my champion and most trusted food critic from day one, long before I even considered a career in food. I can't wait to continue sharing my life with you and to feed our new little family for years to come!

My little Rose, you are not even born yet but I am already overwhelmed with gratitude to have you in my life. You were there from the very beginning of this book making this whole journey even more magical than I could have ever anticipated.

First published in 2019 by

INTERLINK BOOKS
An imprint of Interlink Publishing Group, Inc.
46 Crosby Street, Northampton, MA 01060
www.interlinkbooks.com

Published simultaneously in Great Britain by Mitchell
Beazley, an imprint of Octopus Publishing Group Ltd.
Carmelite House, 50 Victoria Embankment
London, EC4Y 0DZ United Kingdom.

Library of Congress Cataloging-in-Publication
Data available
ISBN: 978-1-62371-921-0

Printed and bound in China
10 9 8 7 6 5 4 3 2 1

Publishing Director Stephanie Jackson
Senior Editor Pauline Bache
American Edition Editor Leyla Moushabeck
Art Director Juliette Norsworthy
Designer Charlotte Heal Design
Photographer Lizzie Mayson
Food Stylist Tamara Vos
Food Stylist (Russia) Alissa Timoshkina
Props Stylist Louie Waller
Senior Production Manager Peter Hunt
American Edition Proofreader Jane Bugaeva

Ovens should be preheated to the specific
temperature. If using a convection oven, follow
manufacturer's instructions for adjusting the time and
the temperature.

Vegetarians should ensure cheeses are made with
vegetarian rennet. There are vegetarian forms of
Parmesan, feta, Cheddar, Cheshire, Red Leicester,
dolcelatte, and many goat cheeses, among others.